AF267431

Critical Thinking for Kids

Understanding Logic, Fallacies, and Smart Decision Making

CONTENTS

PART 1: LOGICAL FALLACIES FOR KIDS

PART 2: DECISION-MAKING FOR KIDS

Part 1: Logical Fallacies for Kids

Outsmart Bad Reasoning and Catch Silly Arguments!

Introduction: Welcome to the World of Logical Fallacies!

Hi there! Did you know your brain is like a superhero? It helps you solve problems, win arguments, and figure out the truth. But even superheroes have weaknesses, and their brains sometimes fall for tricks and traps called logical fallacies.

What's a Logical Fallacy?

It's a fancy way of saying "bad thinking." Logical fallacies happen when arguments don't make sense, even if they sound like they do. They're like sneaky little tricks that confuse people. But don't worry — you're about to learn how to spot them like a pro!

Here's an example:

- Imagine your friend says, "If you don't share your candy, you're a bad person!"
- Wait a second … does not sharing candy really make someone bad? Nope! That's called a fallacy — a bad argument designed to make you feel guilty instead of thinking clearly.

Why Does This Happen?

Humans sometimes fall for fallacies because they're emotional, tired, or just trying to win an argument quickly. But you're smarter than that! By learning about these common mistakes, you'll know when someone's argument doesn't add up.

Why Should You Learn This?

- You'll Outsmart Tricky Arguments: No one will be able to fool you with silly thinking.

- You'll Be a Super Debater: Whether you're talking to friends, family, or anyone else, you'll always have the sharpest mind in the room.

- You'll See the Truth: Knowing what makes a good argument helps you understand the world better — and even helps you make smarter decisions!

How This Book Works

Each chapter in this book will teach you about one fallacy. You'll see funny examples, learn why the fallacy doesn't work, and get tips on how to avoid it. Plus, you'll get some practice so you can become a fallacy-detecting ninja!

Get Ready for a Brain Workout!

By the end of this book, you'll have a powerful new skill: the ability to think clearly, argue fairly, and spot bad reasoning from a mile away. You're about to become the hero of logical thinking — so, grab your cape (or just a comfy chair), and let's jump into the first fallacy!

CHAPTER 1–10
Everyday Arguments

Welcome to "Everyday Arguments!" This is where you'll learn about some sneaky tricks people use when they argue. Sometimes, people make mistakes like attacking someone instead of their idea or pretending there are only two choices. But don't worry — you'll learn how to spot these mistakes and handle them like a pro. Let's get started and have some fun learning!

Chapter 1: The Ad Hominem Fallacy

What Is It?

The Ad Hominem fallacy happens when someone ignores an idea and instead attacks the person who said it.

Here's an example:

- **Kid 1:** "Eating veggies makes you healthy!"
- **Kid 2:** "What do you know? You didn't even eat broccoli yesterday!"

See the problem? Instead of thinking about the idea (*are veggies healthy?*), Kid 2 attacks Kid 1 (*you didn't eat broccoli*). That's Ad Hominem—a way to dodge the idea by pointing fingers.

Why Is This a Mistake?

Whether Kid 1 eats broccoli or not doesn't change if veggies are healthy. The idea is what matters, not the person saying it.

Think of it like this:

- **Idea:** Eating veggies makes you healthy.
- **Person:** Didn't eat broccoli yesterday.

- The person and the idea are *not* the same thing! The truth of the idea doesn't depend on who said it.

Why Do People Do This?

Sometimes, humans get mad or just want to win an argument, so they attack the person instead of thinking about the idea. It's like yelling, "Your shoes are ugly!" during a game of tag — totally unrelated and not helpful.

How to Avoid This Mistake

1. Listen to the idea. Forget about who said it—just think about whether the idea is true.
2. Ask yourself: "Would this idea still be true if someone else said it?"
3. Don't get personal. When you argue back, talk about the *idea*, not the person.

Practice Example

Let's try!

- Your friend says: "Reading every day makes you smarter."
- Instead of saying: "What do you know? You watch cartoons all day!"
- Ask yourself: "Hmm... is it true that reading makes people smarter?"

How to Handle Ad Hominem

If someone attacks you instead of your idea, don't worry! Here's what you can say:

1. **Bring the focus back:** "That's about me, but what do you think about the idea?"
2. **Make it look silly:** "Wow, I must have a strong idea if the only thing to argue about is me!"
3. **Invite them back to the topic:** "Okay, let's leave the personal stuff and talk about the idea instead."
4. **Use humor:** "Cool! Now that we've talked about me, can we talk about the actual point?"

Remember This:

Attacking the person is like throwing spaghetti at the wall — messy and pointless. Instead, stick to the idea, and you'll always be one step closer to the truth.

Chapter 2: The Straw Man Fallacy

What Is It?

The Straw Man fallacy happens when someone changes what you said to make it sound silly, extreme, or wrong, and then argues against that fake version of your idea.

Here's an Example:

- Kid 1: "I think we should play soccer."
- Kid 2: "Oh, so you hate all other sports now?"

Can you tell why this doesn't work? Kid 1 never said they hated other sports, but Kid 2 twisted the idea to make it sound extreme.

Why Is This a Mistake?

It's not fair to argue against something a person didn't actually say. Instead of listening to their real idea, you're arguing with a fake version of it —a "straw man." This doesn't help anyone understand the truth.

Why Do People Do This?

- It's easier to argue against a fake, exaggerated idea.
- They might not fully understand the real argument.
- They want to make their point seem stronger.

How to Avoid This Mistake:

1. Listen carefully to the other person's real idea.
2. Ask questions to make sure you understand: "Are you saying [the idea]?"
3. Respond to the real idea, not a twisted version of it.

Practice Example:

Let's try!

- Friend: "I think we should eat more fruit."
- Instead of saying: "Oh, so you think we should never eat cookies again?"
- Try saying: "Why do you think eating more fruit is a good idea?"

How to Handle the Straw Man Fallacy:

If someone twists your words, here's what you can say:

1. "That's not what I said. Let me explain what I actually meant."
2. "You're changing my words. Let's talk about my real idea instead."
3. "Here's what I really meant—can we focus on that?"

Remember This:

Arguing with a fake version of someone's idea is like fighting a shadow — it's pointless. Stick to the real idea to have a fair and helpful conversation.

Chapter 3: The False Dilemma Fallacy

What Is It?

The False Dilemma fallacy happens when someone makes it seem like there are only two choices, even though there are more options. It's like saying, "You can only have chocolate or vanilla," when there's a whole freezer of ice cream flavors!

Here's an Example:

- Kid 1: "You can either do your homework or never succeed!"
- Kid 2: "Wait, can't I do my homework and still have fun?"

Kid 1 is pretending there are only two choices, but Kid 2 shows that life isn't always so black and white.

Why Is This a Mistake?

Life is full of possibilities, and pretending there are only two choices can make people feel trapped or rushed into making the wrong decision. It's unfair and oversimplifies the situation.

Why Do People Do This?

- They want to make their choice seem better by ignoring other options.
- They don't take time to think about all the possibilities.
- They might want to pressure you into picking a side.

How to Avoid This Mistake

1. Ask, "Are these really the only two choices, or are there more?"
2. Take a moment to explore other ideas or solutions.
3. Don't let anyone rush you into deciding between two things if there might be more options.

Practice Example

Let's try!

- Kid 1: "You can either eat broccoli or go to bed hungry!"
- You: "Wait, what about eating something else, like carrots?"

How to Handle the False Dilemma Fallacy

If someone says you only have two choices, try this:

1. **Point Out Other Options:** "I don't think those are the only choices. Let's look at more ideas."
2. **Ask Questions:** "Why do you think it has to be just this or that?"
3. **Suggest a Middle Ground:** "How about we try both? Or something in between?"

Remember This:

The world isn't just black and white—it's full of colors and possibilities! Don't let someone force you into a choice when there might be lots of other options waiting to be discovered.

Chapter 4: The Bandwagon Fallacy

What Is It?

The Bandwagon fallacy happens when someone says something must be good, right, or true just because a lot of people like it or do it. It's like saying, "Everyone is jumping on this wagon, so it must be the best wagon ever!" But just because something is popular doesn't mean it's the right choice for you.

Here's an Example:

- Kid 1: "Everyone has these shoes, so they must be the best!"
- Kid 2: "Just because everyone has them doesn't mean they're the best for me."

See what's happening? Kid 1 is assuming the shoes are the best simply because they're popular. But Kid 2 knows that being popular doesn't always mean something is good or the right choice for everyone.

Why Is This a Mistake?

Popularity doesn't equal quality. Just because something is popular doesn't mean it's the best choice for you. Crowds can be wrong, and what's right for others might not be right for you. It's important to think for yourself instead of following what everyone else is doing.

Why Do People Do This?

- They want to fit in and be like everyone else.
- They think, "If everyone likes it, it must be great."
- They feel safer following the crowd instead of making their own choice.

How to Avoid This Mistake

1. **Think for Yourself:** Ask, "Do I actually like this, or do I just want to fit in?"
2. **Look for Reasons:** Ask, "Why is this popular? Is it actually good, or do people just think it is?"
3. **Be Brave:** It's okay to make your own choices, even if they're different from the crowd.

Practice Example

Let's try!

- Kid 1: "Everyone in my class says this video game is the best, so it must be!"
- You: "Maybe it's fun, but I want to check out reviews and see if it's something I'd like too."

How to Handle the Bandwagon Fallacy

If someone tries to convince you to follow the crowd, here's what you can say:

1. **Question It:** "Just because everyone's doing it, does that make it the best choice?"
2. **Be Confident:** "I don't need to follow the crowd to make a good decision."
3. **Suggest Thinking Together:** "Let's figure out if it's actually good instead of just popular."

Remember This:

It's okay to be different! What works for others might not work for you, and that's totally fine. Thinking for yourself makes you stronger and more independent, so don't let the crowd decide for you.

Chapter 5: The Appeal to Authority Fallacy

What Is It?

The Appeal to Authority fallacy happens when someone says something must be true just because an "important" or "smart" person said it — even if that person isn't an expert on the topic.

Here's an Example:

- Kid 1: "The best way to win a race is to wear shiny shoes."
- Kid 2: "Why do you think that?"
- Kid 1: "Because my cousin said so, and he's really cool!"

See the problem? Just because Kid 1's cousin is cool doesn't mean they know the best way to win a race. What matters is whether the idea itself makes sense, not who said it.

Why Is This a Mistake?

Good ideas and arguments should be based on facts, not just on who said them. Even smart or famous people can make mistakes or have opinions that aren't backed by proof. What matters most is whether the idea itself is true.

Why Do People Do This?

- They trust the person and assume they must be right.
- They think being smart, cool, or famous makes someone an expert.
- They don't stop to check if the person really knows what they're talking about.

How to Avoid This Mistake

1. Ask: "Is this person really an expert on this topic?"
2. Look for evidence: "Does their idea make sense on its own?"
3. Think for yourself: "Even if I like this person, is their argument logical and true?"

Practice Example

Let's try!

- Kid 1: "This app is the best because a famous YouTuber said so!"
- You: "That's cool, but let's look at reviews to see if it's really good."

How to Handle the Appeal to Authority Fallacy

If someone tells you to believe something just because an important person said it, try this:

1. **Ask Questions:** "How does this person know it's true? Are they an expert?"
2. **Look for Proof:** "Let's check if there's evidence to back this up."
3. **Be Polite but Firm:** "Even if this person is smart, I'd like to learn more about the idea itself."

Remember This:

It's okay to admire someone, but that doesn't mean everything they say is true. Always check the facts and think for yourself. The truth matters more than who said it!

Chapter 6: The Appeal to Emotion Fallacy

What Is It?

The Appeal to Emotion fallacy happens when someone tries to convince you by making you feel something — like guilt, fear, or sadness — rather than giving a good reason. Instead of explaining why their idea is right, they use emotions to push you to agree.

Here's an Example:

- Kid 1: "You should share your tablet because it'll make me happy!"
- Kid 2: "But being happy isn't a reason. Why do you need it?"

What's not adding up? Kid 1 isn't giving a real reason for sharing the tablet. Instead, they're using emotions to make Kid 2 feel bad so they'll give in.

Why Is This a Mistake?

Feelings are important, but they don't prove whether an argument is true or fair. A good argument should be based on reasons and facts, not just emotions. Using emotions might seem powerful, but it's not a fair way to have a discussion.

Why Do People Do This?

- They might not have a strong reason, so they rely on feelings to get their way.

- They know emotions like guilt or fear are hard to ignore.

- They may not realize they're trying to manipulate your feelings instead of explaining their point.

How to Avoid This Mistake

1. **Stay Calm:** Ask yourself, "Is this about facts or feelings?"

2. **Look for a Real Reason:** "Do they have a fair reason, or are they just trying to make me feel something?"

3. **Think Clearly:** Don't let your emotions stop you from making a smart decision.

Practice Example

Let's try!

- Kid 1: "You have to let me copy your homework, or I'll get in trouble!"

- You: "I don't want you to get in trouble, but copying isn't the right solution. Let's figure out how you can finish it yourself."

How to Handle the Appeal to Emotion Fallacy

If someone uses feelings to convince you, here's how you can respond:

1. **Acknowledge Their Feelings:** "I understand that you feel this way."

2. **Shift to the Real Issue:** "But let's talk about the actual reason why this matters."

3. **Be Kind but Firm:** "I care about how you feel, but I also want to make the right choice."

Remember This:

It's okay to care about other people's feelings, but don't let emotions replace good reasoning. Smart decisions are made by thinking clearly, even when feelings are involved.

Chapter 7: The Hasty Generalization Fallacy

What Is It?

The Hasty Generalization fallacy happens when someone makes a big decision or assumption based on just one or a few examples. It's like saying, "I saw one rainy day, so it must rain every day!" without looking at the bigger picture.

Here's an Example:

- Kid 1: "I saw one scary dog, so all dogs must be mean!"
- Kid 2: "That's not true! Most dogs are friendly — you just saw one bad example."

See what's happening? Kid 1 is making a quick judgment about all dogs based on just one scary experience. But Kid 2 knows that one bad example doesn't tell the whole story.

Why Is This a Mistake?

It's unfair to decide something is true about everyone or everything based on just a small sample. You need more information before you can make a smart decision.

Why Do People Do This?

- They jump to conclusions instead of taking time to think.
- They let one bad (or good) experience shape their whole opinion.
- They don't stop to look at the bigger picture or more examples.

How to Avoid This Mistake

1. **Look for More Info:** Ask yourself, "Is this just one example, or do I know more about this?"
2. **Think Bigger:** "Does this really happen all the time, or is this just one situation?"
3. **Stay Open-Minded:** Be willing to admit you might need more facts before deciding.

Practice Example

Let's try!

- Kid 1: "The cafeteria food was bad today, so it must always be terrible!"
- You: "Maybe it's just bad today. Let's try it tomorrow and see if it's different."

How to Handle the Hasty Generalization Fallacy

If someone makes a quick judgment, here's what you can do:

1. **Ask for More Proof:** "Do you have more examples to back this up?"
2. **Point Out the Problem:** "That's just one example—you can't say it's true for everything."
3. **Encourage Patience:** "Let's take our time and look at more cases before deciding."

Remember This:

One example doesn't tell the whole story. Don't jump to conclusions — gather more facts and think carefully before making a big decision.

Chapter 8: The Slippery Slope Fallacy

What Is It?

The Slippery Slope fallacy happens when someone says that if one thing happens, it will lead to a chain of events that ends in something really bad—even if there's no good reason to think that will happen. It's like saying, "If you eat one cookie, you'll end up eating every cookie in the house!"

Here's an Example:

- Kid 1: "If we stay up late tonight, we'll never go to bed on time again!"
- Kid 2: "Why do you think that? Staying up late one time doesn't mean we'll never go to bed on time."

See why this doesn't fit? Kid 1 is assuming that one small action (staying up late) will lead to a huge problem without proof. Kid 2 knows that one choice doesn't always lead to a disaster.

Why Is This a Mistake?

Not every small action leads to a big chain reaction. Life isn't like a slippery slide where one small step means you're out of control. Decisions and events happen step by step, and one choice doesn't automatically mean the worst will happen.

Why Do People Do This?

- They're worried about the future and let their fears take over.
- They exaggerate to make their argument seem stronger.
- They might not realize they're skipping over all the steps in between.

How to Avoid This Mistake

1. **Take a Step Back:** Ask yourself, "Is this really going to lead to such a big problem?"
2. **Think About the Steps:** "What would actually have to happen to get from here to there?"
3. **Look for Proof:** "Do I have evidence that this will really happen?"

Practice Example

Let's try!

- Kid 1: "If we let people chew gum in class, soon everyone will bring snacks, and the classroom will be a mess!"
- You: "Chewing gum doesn't mean snacks will be allowed. Let's see if chewing gum actually causes problems first."

How to Handle the Slippery Slope Fallacy

If someone makes a wild claim about how one small thing will lead to disaster, try this:

1. **Ask for Proof:** "Why do you think this will happen?"
2. **Focus on the Present:** "Let's deal with what's happening right now instead of worrying about what might happen later."
3. **Stay Calm and Logical:** "One small choice doesn't mean everything will fall apart. Let's look at the facts."

Remember This:

Life doesn't slide out of control as easily as people might think. Instead of worrying about the worst-case scenario, focus on what's actually happening and take it one step at a time.

Chapter 9: The Red Herring Fallacy

What Is It?

The Red Herring fallacy happens when someone tries to distract you by changing the subject or bringing up something unrelated. It's like tossing a smelly fish (a "red herring") into the conversation to make you follow a new trail and forget the original point!

Here's an Example:

- Kid 1: "You didn't clean your room like you promised!"
- Kid 2: "Why are you always so mean to me?"

See the trick? Kid 1 wants to talk about cleaning the room, but Kid 2 changes the subject to avoid the issue. Instead of staying on topic, they bring up something unrelated to distract from the real conversation.

Why Is This a Mistake?

Good arguments stick to the point. Changing the subject might make someone forget the original issue, but it doesn't solve anything. It's like trying to win a race by running off the track — distracting, but not helpful.

Why Do People Do This?

- They don't have a good answer to the main topic.
- They want to confuse or distract the other person.
- They feel uncomfortable or nervous about the real issue.

How to Avoid This Mistake

1. **Stay Focused:** Ask, "Is this related to what we were talking about?"

2. **Bring It Back:** "Let's stick to the main point and talk about that first."

3. **Don't Get Distracted:** Think carefully about whether the new topic actually matters.

Practice Example:

Let's try!

- Kid 1: "You didn't share the markers during art class."
- Kid 2: "Well, you were late to class today!"
- You: "Being late isn't the same as sharing markers. Let's talk about sharing."

How to Handle the Red Herring Fallacy:

If someone tries to distract you, here's how you can respond:

1. **Point It Out:** "That's not what we were talking about. Let's get back to the topic."

2. **Ask for Focus:** "Can we stay on track and talk about this first?"

3. **Be Fair but Firm:** "We can talk about your point later, but let's finish this conversation first."

Remember This:

Stay focused! A good argument solves the real problem, not a different one. Don't let distractions lead you off track — stick to the topic and stay calm.

Chapter 10: The Circular Reasoning Fallacy

What Is It?

The Circular Reasoning fallacy happens when someone tries to prove their point by simply repeating it in a different way. It's like running in a circle — you don't get anywhere new! Instead of giving a real reason or proof, they just use the idea itself to explain why it's true.

Here's an Example:

- Kid 1: "This game is fun because it's enjoyable!"
- Kid 2: "But what makes it fun? You're just saying the same thing twice."

Kid 1 isn't giving a real reason for why the game is fun. They're just repeating the same idea using different words.

Why Is This a Mistake?

Good arguments need reasons that explain why something is true. If someone keeps going in circles, they're not adding anything new to the conversation. It might sound like they're making a point, but they're really just repeating themselves.

- They might not realize they're repeating their idea.
- They don't have a strong reason, so they keep saying the same thing in different ways.
- They hope you'll agree if they say it enough times.

How to Avoid This Mistake

1. **Ask Yourself:** "Does this explanation actually prove the idea, or is it just repeating it?"
2. **Look for Real Proof:** "What are the facts or reasons that back this up?"
3. **Take Your Time:** Don't rush to agree if the argument isn't clear or convincing.

Practice Example

Let's try!

- Kid 1: "We have to pick this team because it's the best!"
- You: "Why is it the best? Just saying it's the best doesn't explain why."

How to Handle the Circular Reasoning Fallacy

If someone keeps going in circles, here's how you can respond:

1. **Point It Out:** "You're just repeating the same idea. Can you explain it better?"
2. **Ask for More Details:** "What proof do you have for that?"
3. **Stay Calm:** "I want to understand your point, but you need to give a real reason, not just say the same thing again."

Remember This:

Good arguments move forward, not in circles. Always look for reasons and explanations that make sense and help you understand the idea better.

CHAPTER 11–20
Tricky Thinking

In this section, we'll explore some clever, but sneaky, ways people can make arguments that don't really work. These fallacies might seem tricky at first, but don't worry — you'll learn how to spot them and stay sharp. By the end of this section, you'll know how to handle everything from confusing questions to bad arguments about old traditions or new ideas.

Chapter 11: The Loaded Question Fallacy

What Is It?

The Loaded Question fallacy happens when someone asks a question that unfairly assumes something. No matter how you answer, it feels like you're agreeing to something you didn't mean to. It's like being asked, "Why did you eat all the cookies?" when you didn't eat any!

Here's an Example:

- Kid 1: "Why did you break my toy?"
- Kid 2: "Wait, I didn't break your toy! Let's figure out what happened."

Notice what's tricky here? Kid 1's question already assumes Kid 2 broke the toy, even though that might not be true. It's not fair to frame a question in a way that traps someone.

Why Is This a Mistake?

Loaded questions force people to defend themselves against something that might not even be true. It's unfair because the question assumes something bad, which can make it hard to give an honest answer.

Why Do People Do This?

- They want to trap you into admitting something.
- They think it's easier to win an argument by sneaking in an unfair assumption.
- They might not realize their question is unfair.

How to Avoid This Mistake

1. **Check Your Questions:** Ask yourself, "Am I assuming something that might not be true?"
2. **Be Fair:** Ask clear, honest questions that don't trap the other person.
3. **Stay Open-Minded:** Avoid jumping to conclusions before asking a question.

Practice Example

Let's try!

- Kid 1: "Why are you always mean to me?"
- You: "That's not true. Let's talk about how we can be nicer to each other."

How to Handle the Loaded Question Fallacy

If someone asks you an unfair question, here's what you can do:

1. **Don't Answer Right Away:** "Wait, I don't agree with the way you're asking that."
2. **Challenge the Assumption:** "I don't think that's true. Let's figure out what really happened."
3. **Ask for a Fair Question:** "Can you ask that in a way that doesn't assume I did something wrong?"

Remember This:

You don't have to answer unfair questions. It's okay to point out when someone is making an assumption. Honest conversations start with fair questions, so stay calm and keep the focus on the truth.

Chapter 12: The Gambler's Fallacy

What Is It?

The Gambler's Fallacy happens when someone thinks that what happened before can change what will happen next, even if the two events aren't connected. It's like saying, "The last three coin flips were heads, so the next one must be tails!" But each coin flip is a new chance, and the past flips don't change the odds.

Here's an Example:

- Kid 1: "This coin landed on heads five times in a row, so it has to be tails next!"
- Kid 2: "Nope! The coin still has the same chance to land on heads or tails every time."

See the mistake? Kid 1 is letting the past flips affect their thinking, even though each flip is random and doesn't depend on the last one.

Why Is This a Mistake?

Each event, like flipping a coin or rolling a die, is separate from the ones before it. What happened in the past doesn't change what will happen next. Thinking otherwise can lead to wrong predictions and decisions.

Why Do People Do This?

- They see patterns and think they must mean something.
- They hope they can predict what will happen next.
- They don't realize random events don't follow rules like "balancing out."

How to Avoid This Mistake

1. **Think Logically:** Remind yourself that each chance is separate.
2. **Don't Be Tricked by Patterns:** Just because something happened before doesn't mean it changes the next outcome.
3. **Focus on the Odds:** Look at the real chance of something happening.

Practice Example

Let's try!

- Kid 1: "I've lost five games in a row, so I'm definitely going to win the next one!"
- You: "Winning or losing depends on how you play, not on the last five games."

How to Handle the Gambler's Fallacy

If someone makes this mistake, here's how you can help:

1. **Explain It:** "Each chance is its own thing. What happened before doesn't change what happens next."
2. **Break It Down:** "If the odds are 50/50, they stay the same no matter what happened before."
3. **Stay Patient:** Help them see that patterns in random events don't really mean anything.

Remember This:

Random things don't follow rules like 'balancing out.' Each time is a brand-new chance, so don't let what happened before make you think it changes what comes next.

Chapter 13: The Appeal to Tradition Fallacy

What Is It?

The Appeal to Tradition fallacy happens when someone says something is the best or the right way to do things just because it's been done that way for a long time. It's like saying, "We've always done it this way, so we can't change!" But just because something is old doesn't mean it's the best choice now.

Here's an Example:

- Kid 1: "We always play tag at recess, so we can't play anything else."
- Kid 2: "Why not? Trying a new game could be fun!"

See the problem? Kid 1 is using tradition (always playing tag) as a reason to avoid trying something new. But just because they've always played tag doesn't mean it's the only or best option.

Why Is This a Mistake?

Tradition can be nice, but it's not always the best reason for making decisions. Times change, and new ideas might be better than old ones. If you stick to something just because it's "always been done," you might miss out on better or more exciting choices.

Why Do People Do This?

- They feel safe or comfortable with the way things have always been.
- They don't want to think about new ideas or changes.
- They think "old" automatically means "better" or "right."

How to Avoid This Mistake

1. **Ask Why:** "Why do we do it this way? Is it the best way, or just the old way?"
2. **Be Open to Change:** "Could a new idea work better?"
3. **Think for Yourself:** Don't assume something is right just because it's a tradition.

Practice Example

Let's try!

- Kid 1: "We've always eaten pizza on Fridays, so we can't try something new!"
- You: "Pizza is great, but why not try tacos this Friday and see if we like it?"

How to Handle the Appeal to Tradition Fallacy

If someone says you should do something just because it's a tradition, here's how you can respond:

1. **Question It:** "Just because we've always done it this way, does that mean it's the best way?"
2. **Suggest Something New:** "What if we try a new idea and see how it works?"
3. **Find a Balance:** "We can keep traditions we like, but it's also okay to try new things!"

Remember This:

Traditions can be fun and meaningful, but they aren't always the best reason to make a decision. It's okay to ask questions, think about new ideas, and even start your own traditions. Being open to change helps you grow and learn!

Chapter 14: The Sunk Cost Fallacy

What Is It?

The Sunk Cost fallacy happens when someone keeps doing something just because they've already spent time, money, or effort on it — even if it's not worth it anymore. It's like saying, "I've already eaten half this burned pizza, so I have to eat the rest!" when you could just stop and eat something better.

Here's an Example:

- Kid 1: "I've already spent an hour building this tower, so I can't stop now, even though it keeps falling!"
- Kid 2: "Maybe it's better to start over and build something else that works better."

See the mistake? Kid 1 is sticking with the tower just because they've already spent time on it, even though it might be smarter to start fresh.

Why Is This a Mistake?

Sometimes, we feel like we have to keep going because of what we've already done. But what's already spent — time, effort, or money — can't be changed. Instead of focusing on the past, it's better to think about what will work best moving forward.

Why Do People Do This?

- They don't want to feel like their time or effort was wasted.
- They're too focused on the past to think about what's best for the future.
- They hope things will magically get better if they just keep going.

How to Avoid This Mistake

1. **Think Ahead:** Ask yourself, "Will continuing this make things better, or am I just doing it because of the past?"
2. **Let Go of the Past:** Remember, what's done is done — you can't change it.
3. **Focus on the Future:** Choose what's best for you now, even if it means starting over.

Practice Example

Let's try!

- Kid 1: "I've already spent all my allowance on this broken toy, so I have to keep trying to fix it."
- You: "Maybe it's better to stop and save for something new that actually works."

How to Handle the Sunk Cost Fallacy

If someone is stuck because of what they've already spent, here's what you can say:

1. "What's the best choice moving forward, even if it means letting go of the past?"
2. "It's okay to start over. You'll get better results in the end."
3. "Think about what will make you happiest now, not what you've already done."

Remember This

Don't get stuck because of what you've already spent. Focus on what will help you now and in the future — sometimes starting fresh is the smartest choice.

Chapter 15: The Middle Ground Fallacy

What Is It?

The Middle Ground fallacy happens when someone says the truth must be somewhere in the middle of two sides, even if one side is completely wrong. It's like saying, "If one person says the Earth is flat and another says it's round, it must be half-round and half-flat!"

Here's an Example:

- Kid 1: "We should have homework every single day."
- Kid 2: "We shouldn't have any homework at all."
- Kid 3: "Maybe we should have homework only on weekends."

See the problem? Kid 3 assumes the middle ground is the best choice, but that doesn't mean it's the right one. Sometimes, one side is better than the other!

Why Is This a Mistake?

Just because two sides disagree doesn't mean the answer is in the middle. The truth depends on the facts, not on picking something halfway between two opinions.

Why Do People Do This?

- They think being "fair" means meeting in the middle.
- They don't want to upset anyone, so they compromise even when it doesn't make sense.
- They assume both sides must have equal value.

How to Avoid This Mistake

1. **Look at the Facts:** Ask, "Which side is supported by evidence?"
2. **Be Brave:** It's okay to choose one side if it's the better choice.
3. **Think Clearly:** Don't assume the middle is automatically the best answer.

Practice Example

Let's try!

- Kid 1: "I say we should stay at recess all day."
- Kid 2: "I say we shouldn't have recess at all."
- You: "Let's see what's fair based on the rules instead of just picking the middle."

How to Handle the Middle Ground Fallacy

If someone assumes the middle is always right, here's how you can respond:

1. **Focus on the Facts:** "Let's figure out which idea actually makes sense."
2. **Ask Questions:** "Does the middle choice really solve the problem?"
3. **Stay Fair:** "The middle isn't always best. Let's look at what works instead."

Remember This:

Being in the middle doesn't make something right. The truth depends on the facts, not just picking a spot between two sides.

Chapter 16: The Cherry Picking Fallacy

What Is It?

The Cherry Picking fallacy happens when someone only uses the facts that support their argument and ignores the rest. It's like saying, "This fruit salad is all strawberries!" when you're ignoring the apples, bananas, and grapes.

Here's an Example:

- Kid 1: "This game is the best because it has cool characters!"
- Kid 2: "But what about the bad controls and boring levels?"

Kid 1 is only focusing on one good thing and ignoring the rest. A fair argument should look at all the facts, not just the ones you like.

Why Is This a Mistake?

Focusing on only part of the story doesn't give the full picture. Ignoring important facts can make your argument unfair or misleading.

Why Do People Do This?

- They want their argument to look stronger than it really is.
- They don't want to talk about the bad parts of their idea.
- They think no one will notice the missing information.

How to Avoid This Mistake

1. **Look at Everything:** Ask, "What other facts might I be ignoring?"
2. **Be Honest:** Include both the good and the bad when making your argument.
3. **Think Critically:** Don't let someone convince you with just half the story.

Practice Example

Let's try!

- Kid 1: "This new show is amazing because the main character is funny!"
- You: "That's true, but is the story interesting too? Let's look at the whole picture."

How to Handle the Cherry Picking Fallacy

If someone is only using part of the facts, here's how you can respond:

1. **Ask for the Rest:** "What about the things you didn't mention? Let's look at those too."
2. **Point Out the Problem:** "You're only talking about the good parts, but what about the bad ones?"
3. **Be Fair:** "It's important to look at everything, not just the parts we like."

Remember This:

A fair argument includes all the facts. Don't just pick the "cherries" — look at the whole story to make a smart decision.

Chapter 17: The Appeal to Nature Fallacy

What Is It?

The Appeal to Nature fallacy happens when someone says something is good or right just because it's "natural," or bad just because it's "unnatural." It's like saying, "This candy is bad for you because it isn't made from plants!" without looking at whether the candy is healthy or not.

Here's an Example:

- Kid 1: "You shouldn't use a calculator—it's not natural!"
- Kid 2: "But calculators help solve math problems faster. Isn't that what matters?"

Can you tell what's wrong here? Kid 1 is focusing on whether the calculator is "natural" instead of whether it's useful or helpful.

Why Is This a Mistake?

Just because something is natural doesn't mean it's good, and just because something is unnatural doesn't mean it's bad. For example, natural things like poison ivy can be harmful, while "unnatural" things like medicine can help save lives.

Why Do People Do This?

- They think natural things are always better because they come from nature.
- They want to avoid things that seem strange or unfamiliar.
- They assume "natural" and "good" mean the same thing.

How to Avoid This Mistake

1. **Ask Questions:** "Is this natural thing actually good, or am I just assuming it is?"
2. **Think About the Purpose:** "Does it work or help, whether it's natural or not?"
3. **Focus on the Facts:** Look at what makes something good or bad, not just whether it's natural.

Practice Example

Let's try!

- Kid 1: "This snack is healthier because it's natural."
- You: "Let's check the ingredients and see if it's really good for us."

How to Handle the Appeal to Nature Fallacy

If someone says something is good or bad because of how "natural" it is, you can respond by:

1. **Questioning It:** "What does natural have to do with whether it's good or bad?"
2. **Looking for Proof:** "Let's check if it's actually helpful or harmful."
3. **Staying Open-Minded:** "Natural doesn't always mean good, and unnatural doesn't always mean bad."

Remember This:

What matters is whether something is helpful, safe, or effective—not whether it's natural. Look at the facts, not just the label.

Chapter 18: The Appeal to Consequences Fallacy

What Is It?

The Appeal to Consequences fallacy happens when someone says an idea must be true or false based on whether the result is good or bad, instead of looking at the facts. It's like saying, "This can't be true because I don't like what would happen if it is!"

Here's an Example:

- Kid 1: "If we don't win the soccer game, Coach will be disappointed, so we have to win!"
- Kid 2: "Coach might be disappointed, but that doesn't change whether we win or lose."

Kid 1 is focusing on the consequences of losing instead of the reality of the situation.

Why Is This a Mistake?

Good arguments are based on facts, not just on how the outcome makes you feel. The truth doesn't change just because you like or dislike what it leads to.

- They want to avoid bad outcomes.
- They think emotions or consequences are more important than the facts.
- They might not realize they're letting feelings influence their thinking.

How to Avoid This Mistake

1. **Focus on Facts:** Ask, "Is this true, even if the result isn't what I want?"
2. **Separate Feelings from Truth:** "How I feel about the outcome doesn't change the facts."
3. **Think Clearly:** Don't let fear or hope distract you from the truth.

Practice Example

Let's try!

- Kid 1: "We can't lose this game because it would ruin my day!"
- You: "Losing might be disappointing, but let's focus on playing our best."

How to Handle the Appeal to Consequences Fallacy

If someone lets the result affect how they think, try this

1. **Ask Questions:** "Does the result change whether this is true or false?"
2. **Bring Back the Facts:** "Let's focus on what's real, not just how we feel about it."
3. **Encourage Clear Thinking:** "The outcome matters, but so does figuring out the truth."

Remember This:

The truth stays the same, even if you don't like the results. Focus on facts first, and then think about what to do next.

Chapter 19: The Personal Incredulity Fallacy

What Is It?

The Personal Incredulity fallacy happens when someone says something can't be true just because they don't understand it or find it hard to believe. It's like saying, "I don't get how this works, so it must be fake!"

Here's an Example:

- Kid 1: "How can planes fly? They're so heavy! That can't be real."

- Kid 2: "Just because you don't understand it doesn't mean it's not real. Planes fly because of science and engines!"

See the problem? Kid 1 thinks planes can't fly just because they don't understand how it works. But not understanding something doesn't make it untrue.

Why Is This a Mistake?

The world is full of things we might not fully understand, but that doesn't mean they aren't real. Instead of relying on what you know, it's better to learn more and find out the facts.

Why Do People Do This?

- They feel confused and think something can't be true because they don't get it.
- They assume that if they can't explain it, no one can.
- They might be too quick to dismiss new ideas.

How to Avoid This Mistake

1. **Be Curious:** Ask, "What can I learn about this to understand it better?"
2. **Stay Open-Minded:** "Just because I don't understand it doesn't mean it's wrong."
3. **Look for Answers:** Research or ask questions to find out more about the topic.

Practice Example

Let's try!

- Kid 1: "How can birds fly? That doesn't make sense!"
- You: "Birds can fly because of their wings and how they push against the air. Let's learn more about it together!"

How to Handle the Personal Incredulity Fallacy

If someone says something isn't true because they don't understand it, try this:

1. **Encourage Learning:** "Let's figure out how it works together."
2. **Point Out the Problem:** "Just because you don't get it doesn't mean it's not real."
3. **Stay Positive:** "It's okay to not know everything—we can always learn more!"

Remember This:

Not understanding something doesn't make it untrue. The world is full of amazing things, so stay curious and keep learning!

Chapter 20: The Appeal to Novelty Fallacy

What Is It?

The Appeal to Novelty fallacy happens when someone says something must be better or true just because it's new. It's like saying, "This brand-new toy is the best because it just came out!" But new doesn't always mean better — it's important to look at the facts.

Here's an Example:

- Kid 1: "This new phone is the best because it's the newest model!"
- Kid 2: "But is it really better? Let's check what it can do."

Kid 1 is assuming the phone is the best just because it's new, but Kid 2 knows that being new doesn't automatically make something the best.

Why Is This a Mistake?

Not everything new is better, just like not everything old is bad. New things can have problems, and sometimes older things work just as well—or even better! It's important to check if the new thing is actually an improvement.

Why Do People Do This?

- They get excited about new things because they seem cool or different.
- They assume anything new must be better than what came before.
- They want to keep up with trends and don't want to feel left out.

How to Avoid This Mistake

1. **Check the Details:** Ask, "What makes this new thing better?"
2. **Think Before You Decide:** "Is this really better, or does it just look new and shiny?"
3. **Compare Carefully:** Look at what the new thing can do versus the old one.

Practice Example

Let's try!

- Kid 1: "This new game must be awesome because it just came out!"
- You: "Let's read some reviews to see if it's actually fun to play."

How to Handle the Appeal to Novelty Fallacy

If someone says something is better just because it's new, here's how you can respond:

1. **Ask Questions:** "What makes this better than the old one?"
2. **Look for Evidence:** "Let's check if it's actually improved or just new."
3. **Be Open-Minded:** "New doesn't always mean better — let's find out if it's worth it."

Remember This:

New things can be cool, but they're not always better. What matters is if it works well or is actually improved — not just because it's the newest thing. Take your time to decide before getting too excited about what's new!

CHAPTER 21–30
Sneaky Tricks

This section is all about tricky ways people try to win arguments or convince others, even when their ideas don't really make sense. These fallacies are like little traps that can confuse you if you're not careful. Don't worry — you'll learn how to spot and handle them, so you can stay one step ahead!

Chapter 21: The No True Scotsman Fallacy

What Is It?

The No True Scotsman fallacy happens when someone says, "You're not part of the group because you don't act the way I think you should." It's like saying, "No real fans of this team would cheer for the other side," even though some fans might!

Here's an Example:

- Kid 1: "No true gamer likes puzzle games."
- Kid 2: "But I'm a gamer, and I like puzzle games!"
- Kid 1: "Well, then you're not a true gamer!"

Kid 1 is changing the definition of "gamer" to make their argument work, instead of accepting that different people can have different tastes.

Why Is This a Mistake?

It's not fair to change the rules about who belongs in a group just to win an argument. People in the same group can be different and have their own ideas — and that's totally okay!

- They want their group to seem better or more special.
- They don't like admitting that other opinions exist.
- They believe changing the rules will make their argument seem right.

How to Avoid This Mistake

1. **Be Open-Minded:** Accept that people in a group can have different ideas.
2. **Stick to the Facts:** Don't change definitions just to win an argument.
3. **Respect Others:** Let people define their own interests or identities.

Practice Example

Let's try!

- Kid 1: "No true soccer player would ever play video games!"
- You: "That's not fair. Lots of great soccer players also like video games!"

How to Handle the No True Scotsman Fallacy

If someone tries to exclude you or others with this fallacy, say:

1. "Why does someone have to fit your definition to be part of the group?"
2. "People can have different opinions and still belong to the same group."
3. "Let's focus on the actual topic instead of changing the rules."

Remember This:

Groups can have lots of different people with lots of different ideas. Changing the definition of a group just to win an argument isn't helpful.

Chapter 22: The Texas Sharpshooter Fallacy

What Is It?

The Texas Sharpshooter fallacy happens when someone only pays attention to the facts that make their argument look good and ignores everything else — kind of like drawing a target around the spots where their darts already landed to make it look like they hit the bullseye!

Here's an Example:

- Kid 1: "Our class is the best because we won three awards this year!"
- Kid 2: "But other classes won awards too, and some of them won even more."

Kid 1 is only looking at the good parts and ignoring the rest of the facts.

Why Is This a Mistake?

Only looking at facts that make you seem right doesn't tell the whole story. A good argument needs to include all the facts, even the ones that don't agree with you.

Why Do People Do This?

- They want to make their argument look stronger.
- They don't want to deal with information that disagrees with them.
- They think no one will notice what they left out.

How to Avoid This Mistake

1. **Look at Everything:** Don't ignore facts that don't fit your idea.
2. **Be Honest:** Share the full story, not just the parts that help you.
3. **Ask Questions:** Check if someone is leaving out important information.

Practice Example

Let's try!

- Kid 1: "This snack is the healthiest because it has fruit in it!"
- You: "But it's also full of sugar. Let's look at the whole picture."

How to Handle the Texas Sharpshooter Fallacy

If someone focuses only on certain facts, say:

1. "What about the other information you're leaving out?"
2. "Let's look at all the facts, not just the ones that fit your idea."
3. "It's important to be fair and honest about everything."

Remember This:

Good arguments include the whole story, not just the parts that look good. Always ask for the full picture before deciding what's true.

Chapter 23: The Survivorship Bias Fallacy

What Is It?

The Survivorship Bias fallacy happens when someone only looks at successes and ignores failures. It's like saying, "Anyone can become a famous singer if they practice every day!" without thinking about all the people who practiced hard but never became famous.

Here's an Example:

- Kid 1: "If we practice every day, we'll win the championship because last year's team did!"
- Kid 2: "But what about all the teams that practiced just as much and didn't win?"

What doesn't seem right? Kid 1 is only looking at the team that won and ignoring the others who worked just as hard but didn't succeed.

Why Is This a Mistake?

Focusing only on the winners doesn't give you the full story. Success can teach you valuable lessons, but failures are just as important because they show what didn't work. Ignoring failures might make success seem easier than it really is.

Why Do People Do This?

- Success stories are exciting and easy to remember.
- They want to feel hopeful and inspired, so they ignore failures.
- They assume that copying a winner's actions will guarantee success.

How to Avoid This Mistake

1. **Ask About Failures:** "What happened to the people who tried this and didn't succeed?"
2. **Look at the Bigger Picture:** Success is great, but it's only part of the story.
3. **Be Realistic:** Remember that success isn't always guaranteed, even with hard work.

Practice Example

Let's try!

- Kid 1: "All the best basketball players practiced every day, so if I practice, I'll be a pro too!"
- You: "Practice is important, but not everyone who practices becomes a pro. Let's focus on getting better for now."

How to Handle the Survivorship Bias Fallacy

If someone is only focusing on successes, try this:

1. **Ask Questions:** "What about the people who did the same thing but didn't succeed?"
2. **Show the Whole Picture:** "Success stories are great, but failures can teach us, too."
3. **Be Encouraging:** "You can still work hard and do your best, but remember that success takes more than just copying others."

Remember This

Success stories are inspiring, but they're not the full story. Don't forget to learn from failures—they can teach you just as much (or even more!) about how to improve and make smarter choices.

Chapter 24: The Scare Tactic Fallacy

What Is It?

The Scare Tactic fallacy happens when someone tries to scare you into agreeing with them instead of giving good reasons. It's like saying, "If you don't eat your vegetables, you'll never grow tall!" Scary statements might make you feel worried, but they're not always based on facts.

Here's an Example:

- Kid 1: "If you don't join the soccer team, you'll have no friends!"
- Kid 2: "That's not true! I can still have friends even if I don't play soccer."

Can you tell what's wrong here? Kid 1 is using fear to convince Kid 2, instead of explaining why the soccer team is a good choice.

Why Is This a Mistake?

Fear might grab your attention, but it's not a good reason to make a decision. Scary claims don't always tell the whole truth, and they can push you into making a choice that isn't right for you.

Why Do People Do This?

- They think fear is the easiest way to get someone to agree.
- They don't have strong reasons, so they rely on making you worried.
- They might be scared themselves and want you to feel the same way.

How to Avoid This Mistake

1. **Stay Calm:** Don't let fear stop you from thinking clearly.
2. **Ask Questions:** "Is this fear based on facts, or is it just to scare me?"
3. **Look for Proof:** Make decisions based on good reasons, not just scary ones.

Practice Example

Let's try!

- Kid 1: "If you don't study super hard, you'll fail every test!"
- You: "I'll study because it helps me learn, not because I'm scared of failing."

How to Handle the Scare Tactic Fallacy

If someone tries to scare you into agreeing with them, say:

1. "Why do you think that will happen? Can you explain more?"
2. "I'm not going to decide based on fear—I want to know the real reasons."
3. "Scary doesn't always mean true. Let's look at the facts instead."

Remember This:

Fear can feel powerful, but it doesn't mean something is true. Take a deep breath, think carefully, and make decisions based on reasons, not just scary words.

Chapter 25: The Appeal to Personal Experience Fallacy

What Is It?

The Appeal to Personal Experience fallacy happens when someone says their own experience is proof of something being true for everyone. It's like saying, "This snack is the best because I like it!" Your experience is important, but it's not always enough to prove something for everyone.

Here's an Example:

- Kid 1: "I've never seen a shooting star, so they must not be real."

- Kid 2: "Just because you haven't seen one doesn't mean they don't exist."

Do you see the mix-up? Kid 1 is using their own experience to decide what's true, but Kid 2 knows that one person's experience isn't enough to prove something for everyone.

Why Is This a Mistake?

One person's experience is just a single piece of the puzzle. The world is big, and different people have different experiences. A good argument looks at more than just one person's point of view.

Why Do People Do This?

- They believe their own experience because it feels real to them.
- They think if something happened to them, it must happen to everyone.
- They don't always realize that other people's experiences might be different.

How to Avoid This Mistake

1. **Think Bigger:** Ask, "Could other people's experiences be different from mine?"
2. **Look for Evidence:** "What else can we learn about this beyond just my experience?"
3. **Stay Open-Minded:** Be willing to accept that your experience might not tell the whole story.

Practice Example

Let's try!

- Kid 1: "I've never gotten sick from not washing my hands, so it's not important."
- You: "Just because you haven't gotten sick doesn't mean it can't happen. Let's check what doctors say."

How to Handle the Appeal to Personal Experience Fallacy

If someone says their experience proves something, you can respond:

1. "Your experience is important, but it might not be true for everyone."
2. "Let's look at other people's experiences and see what they say."
3. "One story doesn't tell the whole truth—let's check the facts."

Remember This

Your experience matters, but it's not the whole picture. To understand something fully, you need to look at many experiences and facts, not just your own.

Chapter 26: The Composition Fallacy

Great Puzzle Pieces | The Full Puzzle

What Is It?

The Composition fallacy happens when someone assumes that if one part of something is true, it must be true for the whole thing. It's like saying, "This puzzle piece is blue, so the whole puzzle must be blue!"

Here's an Example:

- Kid 1: "My favorite player is on this team, so the whole team must be amazing!"
- Kid 2: "But what about the rest of the players? One person doesn't make a whole team great."

What's the issue here? Kid 1 is judging the whole team based on just one player, but Kid 2 knows you have to look at everything to decide.

Why Is This a Mistake?

One part of something doesn't always tell you about the whole. A good argument looks at all the parts together, not just one piece.

- They think the best part represents everything.
- They don't take the time to look at all the details.
- They get excited about one thing and forget to check the rest.

How to Avoid This Mistake

1. **Look at the Whole Picture:** Don't judge the whole based on one piece.
2. **Ask Questions:** "What are the other parts like? Do they match this one?"
3. **Think Carefully:** Take your time to check all the details before deciding.

Practice Example

Let's try!

- Kid 1: "This book has a cool cover, so the whole story must be awesome!"
- You: "The cover is nice, but let's read a little to see if the story is good too."

How to Handle the Composition Fallacy

If someone judges the whole based on one part, you can say:

1. "That one part is great, but what about the rest?"
2. "Let's check all the pieces before we decide."
3. "One good piece doesn't mean the whole thing is amazing."

Remember This:

The best way to judge something is by looking at all the parts, not just one. Don't let one shiny piece trick you into thinking the whole thing is perfect!

Chapter 27: The Division Fallacy

What Is It?

The Division fallacy happens when someone thinks that what's true for the whole thing must also be true for every little part. It's like saying, "This cake is yummy, so every ingredient must taste yummy too!"

Here's an Example:

- Kid 1: "Our soccer team is the best, so every player must be the best too!"
- Kid 2: "Not every player has to be the best for the team to be great. It's about teamwork!"

Do you spot what's wrong? Kid 1 thinks every part of the team must be amazing just because the whole team is great, but Kid 2 knows that's not always true.

Why Is This a Mistake?

Sometimes the whole is great because of how the parts work together, not because every single part is perfect. Judging the pieces based on the whole can lead to wrong ideas.

Why Do People Do This?

- They think the greatness of the whole automatically applies to every part.
- They don't look at each part separately.
- They want to believe everything about the group is equally good.

How to Avoid This Mistake

1. **Look Closely:** Ask, "Does this part actually match the whole?"
2. **Check the Details:** Think about each piece individually.
3. **Think Clearly:** Remember, something can be great as a whole without every part being amazing.

Practice Example

Let's try!

- Kid 1: "This movie is awesome, so every single scene must be perfect!"
- You: "The movie is great, but maybe some parts are stronger than others."

How to Handle the Division Fallacy

If someone assumes the parts are just like the whole, you can say:

1. "Let's look at each part to see if it's the same as the whole."
2. "The group can be great without every part being perfect."
3. "What makes the whole special might be how the parts work together."

Remember This

Great things are often made up of different pieces, and not all of them have to be perfect. Always take a closer look at each part!

Chapter 28: The Appeal to Hypocrisy (Tu Quoque) Fallacy

What Is It?

The Appeal to Hypocrisy fallacy happens when someone tries to ignore the argument by saying, "You do the same thing!" It's like saying, "You can't tell me not to litter because you littered once too!"

Here's an Example:

- Kid 1: "You shouldn't eat so much candy—it's bad for you."
- Kid 2: "Why should I listen to you? You ate candy yesterday!"

What's off here? Kid 2 is ignoring Kid 1's advice by pointing out something Kid 1 did in the past. But just because someone else isn't perfect doesn't mean their advice is wrong.

Why Is This a Mistake?

This fallacy distracts from the real argument. Instead of focusing on whether the advice is good, it turns the conversation into pointing fingers, which doesn't solve anything.

Why Do People Do This?

- They try to avoid talking about the real issue.
- They think if they point out a mistake you made, they don't have to listen to your advice.
- It's easier to blame someone else than to think carefully about the argument.

How to Avoid This Mistake

1. **Focus on the Argument:** Ask, "Is the advice good, no matter who says it?"
2. **Don't Get Distracted:** Stick to the topic instead of talking about the person.
3. **Stay Fair:** Just because someone isn't perfect doesn't mean their argument isn't valid.

Practice Example

Let's try!

- Kid 1: "You should recycle more to help the planet."
- You: "Even if you forgot to recycle last week, that doesn't mean recycling isn't important."

How to Handle the Appeal to Hypocrisy Fallacy

If someone tries this fallacy, you can say:

1. "Let's focus on the idea, not what the other person did."
2. "Even if someone isn't perfect, their advice can still be helpful."
3. "It's not about who said it—it's about whether it's a good idea."

Remember This:

Pointing fingers doesn't solve anything. Focus on the idea itself and decide if it's good or not, no matter who said it.

Chapter 29: The Appeal to Pity Fallacy

What Is It?

The Appeal to Pity fallacy happens when someone tries to win an argument by making you feel sorry for them instead of giving good reasons. It's like saying, "You have to let me win this game because I had a bad day!"

Here's an Example:

- Kid 1: "I should get extra time on my homework because my dog was barking all night."
- Kid 2: "I'm sorry your dog kept you up, but we all have the same deadline."

Notice what's wrong? Kid 1 is asking for extra time not because of the homework but because of their situation. While it's okay to feel sympathy, it doesn't mean the rules should change.

Why Is This a Mistake?

Feeling bad for someone doesn't make their argument true. Sympathy is important, but it's not a reason to ignore facts or rules.

Why Do People Do This?

- They hope emotions will make you agree with them.
- They don't have strong reasons, so they use pity instead.
- They think making you feel sorry will help them get what they want.

How to Avoid This Mistake

1. **Be Kind but Fair:** Feel sympathy, but don't let it change the facts.
2. **Ask for Reasons:** "Why should we do this, other than feeling bad?"
3. **Stick to the Topic:** Focus on the issue, not the emotions.

Practice Example

Let's try!

- Kid 1: "You should trade snacks with me because I forgot mine at home."
- You: "I feel bad that you forgot your snack, but we need to make a fair trade."

How to Handle the Appeal to Pity Fallacy

If someone uses pity to convince you, try this:

1. "I understand how you feel, but we need to look at the facts too."
2. "Let's think about what's fair for everyone."
3. "Feeling bad for someone doesn't always mean they're right."

Remember This:

It's okay to feel sympathy, but emotions aren't a reason to ignore facts or make decisions. Be kind, but think clearly!

Chapter 30: The False Equivalence Fallacy

What Is It?

The False Equivalence fallacy happens when someone says two things are the same, even though they're very different. It's like saying, "Apples and oranges are the same because they're both fruits!" Sure, they're both fruits, but they're not the same in other ways — they taste different, look different, and grow in different places.

Here's an Example:

- Kid 1: "Getting a bad grade on a test is just as bad as failing the whole class!"
- Kid 2: "Not really! One bad grade can be fixed, but failing the whole class is a much bigger deal."

Can you see what's wrong here? Kid 1 is treating two very different things as if they're equal, but Kid 2 knows they're not the same.

Why Is This a Mistake?

When you treat two things as equal when they're not, it can confuse people and make your argument unfair. Real decisions and problems need to be looked at carefully to see what's really similar and what's not.

Why Do People Do This?

- They want to make their argument sound stronger by comparing it to something bigger or more serious.
- They don't take the time to notice the differences between the two things.
- They might not realize they're comparing two things that aren't truly alike.

How to Avoid This Mistake

1. **Look Closely:** Ask, "Are these two things really the same, or are they just a little similar?"
2. **Be Honest:** Think about the differences as well as the similarities.
3. **Explain Clearly:** Make sure your argument is based on fair comparisons.

Practice Example

Let's try!

- Kid 1: "Not finishing my chores is just as bad as breaking a rule!"
- You: "They're both important, but breaking a rule is usually more serious than forgetting a chore."

How to Handle the False Equivalence Fallacy

If someone tries to compare two things that aren't really the same, you can say:

1. "They're not the same — here's why."
2. "Let's look at how these two things are different."
3. "It's not fair to compare them if they're not alike in important ways."

Remember This:

Not all things that seem similar are actually the same. Look closely, think carefully, and make sure your comparisons are fair and true!

CHAPTER 31 – 40
Deceptive Arguments

Let's explore tricky ways people try to win arguments or make their ideas seem right, even when they're not! These fallacies may sound convincing at first, but once you learn to spot them, they're easy to see through. Get ready to uncover these sneaky tricks and learn how to think clearly and fairly.

Chapter 31: The Genetic Fallacy

What Is It?

The Genetic Fallacy happens when someone says an idea is good or bad just because of where it came from, not because of what it's about. It's like saying, "This game must be bad because it's made by a small company!" The origin of something doesn't always tell you if it's good or bad.

Here's an Example:

- Kid 1: "That toy can't be fun—it's from a store I don't like!"
- Kid 2: "But have you tried it? The store doesn't decide if the toy is fun or not."

What's wrong here? Kid 1 is judging the toy based on where it came from instead of whether it's actually fun.

Why Is This a Mistake?

Where something comes from doesn't always tell you how good or bad it is. Judging ideas or things based only on their source can make you miss out on something great—or believe in something that isn't.

Why Do People Do This?

- They assume the source tells the whole story.
- They want to quickly decide if something is good or bad without looking deeper.
- They trust or dislike certain sources and let that decide for them.

How to Avoid This Mistake

1. **Focus on the Idea:** Ask, "Is this thing good or bad because of what it is, not where it came from?"

2. **Be Curious:** Learn more about the idea itself, not just its source.

3. **Give Things a Chance:** Don't dismiss something without checking it out first.

Practice Example

Let's try!

- Kid 1: "That book can't be good—it's from the library's old section!"
- You: "Let's read a little and see if the story is fun, no matter where it's from."

How to Handle the Genetic Fallacy

If someone says an idea is bad just because of where it came from, you can respond:

1. "Let's look at the idea itself, not just its source."
2. "Where something comes from doesn't always tell the whole story."
3. "The source isn't the only thing that matters—let's check the facts!"

Remember This:

Where something starts doesn't always decide how good or bad it is. Take the time to think about the idea itself!

Chapter 32: The Argument from Silence Fallacy

What Is It?

The Argument from Silence fallacy happens when someone assumes something is true or false just because there's no information about it. It's like saying, "Nobody told me I have homework, so there must not be any!" But just because you haven't heard anything doesn't mean something isn't real or true. Sometimes, silence just means there isn't enough information yet.

Here's an Example:

- Kid 1: "Nobody mentioned a test tomorrow, so we must not have one."

- Kid 2: "But that doesn't mean there's no test. Maybe the teacher just forgot to remind us."

Can you see what's tricky here? Kid 1 is deciding there's no test based on no information at all, but Kid 2 knows that silence doesn't prove anything.

Why Is This a Mistake?

Silence doesn't mean something is true or false—it just means nobody has said anything about it. Making assumptions based on no information can lead to confusion or wrong decisions.

Why Do People Do This?

- They feel impatient and want to fill in the blanks.
- They think that no news must mean something specific.
- They don't realize that silence often means there's not enough information yet.

How to Avoid This Mistake

1. **Wait for More Facts:** Give yourself time to find out the truth before deciding.
2. **Ask Questions:** Try to find evidence instead of making guesses.
3. **Be Comfortable Not Knowing:** It's okay to admit when you don't have all the answers yet.

Practice Example

Let's try!

- Kid 1: "Nobody said I can't bring toys to class, so it must be okay!"
- You: "But that doesn't mean it's allowed. Let's check the class rules to be sure."

How to Handle the Argument from Silence Fallacy

If someone tries to make a point based on no information, you can say:

1. "Just because no one mentioned it doesn't mean it's true or false."
2. "Let's look for real proof instead of guessing."
3. "Sometimes silence just means we don't know yet."

Remember This:

Silence doesn't give you an answer. Not knowing is okay — what matters is finding the facts before making up your mind.

Chapter 33: The Appeal to Probability Fallacy

What Is It?

The Appeal to Probability fallacy happens when someone says something *will* happen just because it *could* happen. It's like saying, "It's possible I'll find money on the ground today, so I definitely will!" Sure, it could happen, but that doesn't mean it's guaranteed. Possibility and certainty are not the same thing.

Here's an Example:

- Kid 1: "I might win the school raffle, so I'm going to win!"
- Kid 2: "It's great to hope, but just because you could win doesn't mean you definitely will."

What's off here? Kid 1 is treating a possibility like it's a sure thing, but Kid 2 knows that just because something can happen doesn't mean it will.

Why Is This a Mistake?

Thinking that something is certain just because it's possible can lead to disappointment or bad decisions. Life is full of possibilities, but not all of them happen. It's important to look at the chances and be realistic.

Why Do People Do This?

- They confuse "could happen" with "will happen."
- They get excited about something they want and assume it's a sure thing.
- They don't think about other possibilities that might stop it from happening.

How to Avoid This Mistake

1. **Think About the Chances:** Ask yourself, "What are the odds of this actually happening?"
2. **Be Realistic:** Remember that possibilities are not guarantees.
3. **Plan for Different Outcomes:** Hope for the best but be ready for other results too.

Practice Example

Let's try!

- Kid 1: "If I study hard, I'll always get an A!"
- You: "Studying is super important, but sometimes other things, like how hard the test is, can make a difference."

How to Handle the Appeal to Probability Fallacy

If someone assumes something will happen just because it can, you can say:

1. "It's possible, but that doesn't mean it's certain."
2. "Let's look at how likely it is instead of just hoping."
3. "It's smart to plan for all the different ways things might go."

Remember This:

Life is full of possibilities, but not all of them will happen. It's great to dream and hope, but always check the facts and stay realistic!

Chapter 34: The Fallacy of Relative Privation

What Is It?

The Fallacy of Relative Privation happens when someone tries to say a problem doesn't matter just because there's something worse. It's like saying, "Why are you upset about your broken toy when there are kids who don't have toys at all?" Sure, there might be bigger problems, but that doesn't mean smaller ones aren't important too.

Here's an Example:

- Kid 1: "I feel sad because I lost my favorite book."
- Kid 2: "Why are you sad? Some kids don't even have books!"

See what's happening? Kid 2 is ignoring Kid 1's feelings by pointing out something else. Just because there are bigger problems doesn't mean Kid 1's feelings don't matter.

Why Is This a Mistake?

Every problem deserves attention, no matter how small it seems. Comparing problems can make people feel like their concerns don't matter, which isn't fair or helpful.

Why Do People Do This?

- They think focusing on bigger problems is more important.
- They might not know how to help with smaller problems.
- They don't realize that all problems, big or small, are important to the person facing them.

How to Avoid This Mistake

1. **Listen First:** Pay attention to the problem without comparing it to others.
2. **Show Empathy:** Remember that everyone's struggles matter.
3. **Help Where You Can:** Focus on solving the problem instead of dismissing it.

Practice Example

Let's try!

- Kid 1: "I'm upset because I got a bad grade on my test."
- You: "I understand why you're upset. Let's think about how to improve next time!"

How to Handle the Fallacy of Relative Privation

If someone dismisses your problem by saying it's small, you can say:

1. "Just because something is smaller doesn't mean it's not important."
2. "All problems matter to the person dealing with them."
3. "We can care about both big and small problems!"

Remember This:

Big problems don't cancel out smaller ones. Everyone's feelings and challenges are important and deserve care and attention.

Chapter 35: The Appeal to Force Fallacy

What Is It?

The Appeal to Force fallacy happens when someone tries to win an argument by threatening or scaring you instead of giving good reasons. It's like saying, "If you don't agree with me, I won't invite you to my party!" Threats might make someone agree, but they don't make the argument true or fair.

Here's an Example:

- Kid 1: "You have to let me go first, or I won't play with you anymore!"
- Kid 2: "That's not fair! Give me a real reason why you should go first."

See the problem? Kid 1 is using a threat to get what they want instead of giving a good reason.

Why Is This a Mistake?

Arguments should be based on facts and fairness, not fear or threats. Using force or intimidation doesn't make someone's point right—it just pressures others to agree.

Why Do People Do This?

- They don't have strong reasons, so they rely on threats.
- They want to control the situation.
- They think fear is the fastest way to win an argument.

How to Avoid This Mistake

1. **Stay Calm:** Don't let fear make your decisions.
2. **Ask for Reasons:** Say, "Can you explain why instead of threatening me?"
3. **Stand Up for Fairness:** Don't give in to threats—focus on what's right.

Practice Example

Let's try!

- Kid 1: "If you don't give me your toy, I'll tell everyone you're mean!"
- You: "That's not a fair reason. Let's figure out how to share instead."

How to Handle the Appeal to Force Fallacy

If someone uses threats, you can respond:

1. "Threats don't make something right — let's talk about it."
2. "You're scaring me, but that doesn't mean I agree."
3. "Let's solve this fairly without using force."

Remember This:

Fair arguments don't use fear or force. Stick to facts and fairness, and don't let threats decide what's right.

Chapter 36: The Appeal to Flattery Fallacy

What Is It?

The Appeal to Flattery fallacy happens when someone tries to convince you by saying something nice instead of giving a good reason. It's like saying, "You're so smart, so you should do my homework for me!" Compliments are great, but they don't make a bad argument true.

Here's an Example:

- Kid 1: "You're the fastest runner in school! Can you clean up for me since you're so good at everything?"
- Kid 2: "Thanks for the compliment, but I'm not doing your clean-up."

What's tricky here? Kid 1 is using flattery to get help, but Kid 2 knows that being complimented doesn't mean they have to agree.

Why Is This a Mistake?

Flattery can feel good, but it doesn't replace real reasons. Using compliments to convince someone can be sneaky and unfair.

Why Do People Do This?

- They think being nice will get them what they want.
- They don't have a strong argument, so they try to charm you instead.
- They hope you won't notice that the compliment isn't related to the request.

How to Avoid This Mistake

1. **Enjoy the Compliment:** Say thank you, but think carefully about the request.
2. **Check the Argument:** Ask, "Does the compliment have anything to do with what they're asking?"
3. **Stick to the Facts:** Don't agree just because of flattery—look for real reasons.

Practice Example

Let's try!

- Kid 1: "You're so good at drawing! Can you do my art project for me?"
- You: "Thanks, but I think you should do your project yourself to learn!"

How to Handle the Appeal to Flattery Fallacy

If someone uses flattery, you can say:

1. "Thanks for the compliment, but what's the real reason?"
2. "Being nice doesn't change what's fair."
3. "I appreciate that, but let's focus on the actual argument."

Remember This:

Compliments are nice, but they don't make a bad argument true. Always think carefully before agreeing!

Chapter 37: The False Attribution Fallacy

What Is It?

The False Attribution fallacy happens when someone uses the name of an expert, source, or fact to make their argument seem true — even if that source isn't reliable or doesn't actually support their point. It's like saying, "This book says dogs can talk, so it must be true!" Just because something sounds official doesn't mean it's accurate.

Here's an Example:

- Kid 1: "I read on a blog that eating only candy is healthy!"
- Kid 2: "Just because a blog said it doesn't mean it's true. Let's check with a doctor or a reliable source."

What's wrong here? Kid 1 is trusting a random source without checking if it's reliable. Kid 2 knows it's important to double-check where the information comes from.

Why Is This a Mistake?

Not all sources can be trusted. If you believe something just because it sounds fancy or important, you could end up believing or sharing something that isn't true.

Why Do People Do This?

- They think attaching a name or source makes their argument stronger.
- They don't check if the source is actually reliable.
- They want to make their argument sound more convincing.

How to Avoid This Mistake

1. **Check the Source:** Ask, "Is this source trustworthy and accurate?"
2. **Look for Proof:** See if other reliable sources agree.
3. **Don't Be Fooled by Names:** Just because something sounds official doesn't mean it's true.

Practice Example:

Let's try!

- Kid 1: "This magazine said unicorns are real!"
- You: "That sounds fun, but let's check if other reliable sources agree."

How to Handle the False Attribution Fallacy

If someone uses a source that doesn't seem reliable, you can say:

1. "Let's check if this source is trustworthy."
2. "Can we find more reliable information to back this up?"
3. "Not all sources are accurate — let's dig deeper."

Remember This:

Not all sources can be trusted. Make sure to double-check information, even if it sounds fancy or important — it might not be true!

Chapter 38: The Broken Window Fallacy

What Is It?

The Broken Window fallacy happens when someone thinks a bad event is actually good because it creates something new. It's like saying, "It's good that the window broke because now we get to fix it!" Fixing the window might help, but the breaking part was still bad!

Here's an Example:

- Kid 1: "It's great that my bike tire popped because now I'll get a new one!"
- Kid 2: "Getting a new tire is helpful, but it would've been better if the tire hadn't popped at all."

What's tricky here? Kid 1 is focusing only on the good thing that came afterward, but Kid 2 knows it's better to avoid the bad thing in the first place.

Why Is This a Mistake?

Bad events don't become good just because something positive happens later. It's important to look at the whole picture, not just the outcome.

Why Do People Do This?

- They want to focus on the positive side of a bad situation.
- They forget that the bad event wasn't necessary for the good thing to happen.
- They confuse the result with the cause.

How to Avoid This Mistake

1. **Think About the Cause:** Ask, "Was the bad event really needed for this good thing to happen?"
2. **Separate the Bad and Good:** Focus on how to avoid bad events while still finding solutions.
3. **Look at the Bigger Picture:** Don't let the outcome overshadow the original problem.

Practice Example

Let's try!

- Kid 1: "It's great that I spilled my juice because now I get a new cup!"
- You: "Getting a new cup is nice, but it's better to avoid spilling the juice in the first place."

How to Handle the Broken Window Fallacy

If someone says a bad event is good because of what comes after, you can say:

1. "The good outcome doesn't erase the bad event."
2. "Let's focus on how to avoid the bad event next time."
3. "It's great to find solutions, but the problem is still a problem."

Remember This:

Good things can come after bad events, but that doesn't make the bad event good. Always look at the full story!

Chapter 39: The Appeal to Common Sense Fallacy

What Is It?

The Appeal to Common Sense fallacy happens when someone says something must be true just because it sounds obvious. It's like saying, "Everyone knows this is the right answer!" But sometimes, what feels obvious isn't actually true, and you need real evidence to back it up.

Here's an Example:

- Kid 1: "It's common sense that plants grow faster if you talk to them!"
- Kid 2: "That sounds interesting, but let's look for proof to see if it's really true."

See the problem? Kid 1 is relying on what "everyone knows," but Kid 2 knows it's important to check if the idea is actually true.

Why Is This a Mistake?

Not everything that seems obvious is correct. Assuming something is true just because it feels right can stop you from finding the real facts.

Why Do People Do This?

- They trust their instincts without checking the facts.
- They think if an idea is popular, it must be true.
- They don't realize that "common sense" can be wrong.

How to Avoid This Mistake

1. **Ask for Evidence:** Say, "What proof do we have for this?"
2. **Think Critically:** Don't assume something is true just because it feels right.
3. **Look for Facts:** Check if the idea is supported by real information.

Practice Example

Let's try!

- Kid 1: "It's common sense that cold weather makes you sick!"
- You: "Cold weather feels bad, but let's check if it really causes sickness."

How to Handle the Appeal to Common Sense Fallacy

If someone says something is true because it's "obvious," you can say:

1. "Just because it seems obvious doesn't mean it's true — let's check it out."
2. "What feels right might not always be right — let's look for proof."
3. "Common sense is a good guess, but facts are what really matter."

Remember This:

Just because something feels obvious doesn't mean it's correct. Take a moment to check the facts and think it through before making up your mind!

Chapter 40: The False Balance Fallacy

What Is It?

The False Balance fallacy happens when someone treats two sides of an argument as if they're equally true or valid — even when one side clearly has stronger evidence. It's like saying, "Let's hear both sides: the idea that the Earth is round and the idea that it's flat." Sure, everyone can have an opinion, but not all opinions are backed by facts.

Here's an Example:

- Kid 1: "Some people say eating only candy is healthy!"
- Kid 2: "Just because some people say that doesn't mean it's as true as eating fruits and veggies!"

Can you spot the mistake? Kid 1 is giving equal weight to two ideas, even though one has much stronger evidence. Kid 2 knows that facts should matter more than just opinions.

Why Is This a Mistake?

Not all ideas are equally true or backed by evidence. Treating them as if they are can confuse people and make bad ideas seem better than they are.

Why Do People Do This?

- They want to be fair and let both sides share their ideas.
- They don't know that one side might have more proof than the other.
- They think all opinions are equally true, even when some don't have facts to back them up.

How to Avoid This Mistake

1. **Check the Evidence:** Ask, "Which side has more facts to back it up?"
2. **Don't Confuse Opinions with Facts:** Remember, just because someone says something doesn't make it true.
3. **Be Fair but Smart:** Listening to both sides is good, but facts should decide what's right.

Practice Example

Let's try!

- Kid 1: "Some people think you don't need to wear a helmet when riding a bike."
- You: "That's their opinion, but the facts show helmets keep us safer, so we should wear them!"

How to Handle the False Balance Fallacy

If someone treats two sides as equally true when they're not, you can say:

1. "Let's check which side has stronger evidence."
2. "Opinions are fine, but facts are what matter most."
3. "It's okay to listen to both sides, but the truth isn't always in the middle."

Remember This:

Being fair doesn't mean all ideas are equally true. Always look for the facts and let the strongest evidence guide your thinking!

CHAPTER 41–50
Advanced Fallacies (Made Easy!)

Hey there, logical thinker! You're doing amazing so far! This section is like leveling up in a game — here, you'll learn about some tricky fallacies that can fool even the smartest people. Don't worry, though! We'll break everything down and keep it fun, so you'll know how to spot these sneaky tricks.

Chapter 41: The Just-World Fallacy

What Is It?

The Just-World fallacy happens when someone believes that life is always fair — like thinking, "Good things only happen to good people, and bad things only happen to bad people." But life doesn't always work that way. Sometimes, bad things happen to good people, and good things happen to people who don't deserve them.

Here's an Example:

- Kid 1: "That kid got detention — they must have done something bad."
- Kid 2: "Maybe, but it's also possible they didn't do anything wrong. Let's find out what happened."

What's happening here? Kid 1 is assuming that life is balanced for everyone, but Kid 2 knows that sometimes people get into trouble even when it's not their fault. It's not always about who deserves what — it could be about something else entirely.

Why Is This a Mistake?

Believing that the world is perfect can make you miss the bigger picture. Sometimes things happen because of bad luck, mistakes, or circumstances that are out of anyone's control.

Why Do People Do This?

- They want to feel safe, thinking bad things only happen if someone deserves it.
- It's easier to blame someone than to think about other reasons for what happened.
- Believing life is fair makes the world feel more predictable.

How to Avoid This Mistake

1. **Ask Questions:** Instead of assuming, ask, "What else could explain this?"
2. **Think About Luck:** Remember that bad luck can happen to anyone, even if they didn't do anything wrong.
3. **Be Kind:** Instead of blaming, think about how you can help or understand the situation better.

Practice Example

Let's try!

- Kid 1: "That kid fell off their bike because they're clumsy."
- You: "Maybe, or maybe they hit a rock they didn't see."

How to Handle the Just-World Fallacy

If someone says something unfair because they believe the world is always just, you can say:

1. "Sometimes bad things happen to good people — it's not their fault."
2. "Let's think about other reasons why this could have happened."
3. "Life isn't always fair, but we can still try to make it better."

Remember This:

The world isn't flawless, and that's okay. What matters is looking for the real reasons behind what happens and being kind to others. Understanding this can help you be more compassionate and a better problem-solver!

Chapter 42: The Ludic Fallacy

What Is It?

The Ludic Fallacy happens when someone assumes that life works like a game, where every rule is clear and every outcome is predictable. But life isn't always that simple! In real life, unexpected things can happen, and not everything follows a set of rules.

Here's an Example:

- Kid 1: "If I practice soccer for one hour every day, I'll definitely become a pro!"
- Kid 2: "Practice is great, but other things, like teamwork and opportunities, matter too."

See the problem? Kid 1 thinks life works like a step-by-step guide, but Kid 2 knows there's more to it.

Why Is This a Mistake?

Thinking life is like a game can make you miss out on surprises or other important factors. Life is messy and full of unknowns. Believing everything is predictable can lead to wrong expectations or disappointment.

Why Do People Do This?

- They like things to be neat and simple.
- They believe following the "rules" always leads to success.
- They want to feel in control of outcomes.

How to Avoid This Mistake

1. **Expect the Unexpected:** Remember, life doesn't always follow the rules you expect.
2. **Look at the Bigger Picture:** Think about all the factors that might affect a situation.
3. **Stay Flexible:** Be ready to adjust when things don't go as planned.

Practice Example

Let's try!

- Kid 1: "If I wear my lucky socks, I'll win the game!"
- You: "Maybe, but practicing and working as a team are what really help us win."

How to Handle the Ludic Fallacy

If someone thinks life works like a game, you can say:

1. "Life's not always that simple — let's think about what else could happen."
2. "There's more to life than following one rule."
3. "It's great to have a plan, but we also need to stay flexible."

Remember This:

Life isn't a game, and that's okay! Being open to surprises and thinking about all the possibilities helps you handle whatever comes your way.

Chapter 43: The Pro-Innovation Bias Fallacy

What Is It?

The Pro-Innovation Bias happens when someone thinks new things are always better, just because they're new. It's like thinking, "This new game is the best ever!" without checking if it's actually fun or better than the old one.

Here's an Example:

- Kid 1: "This new toy must be the best—it just came out!"
- Kid 2: "Let's try it first to see if it's actually better than what we already have."

What's happening? Kid 1 is overly excited about something new, but Kid 2 knows it's important to test it out before deciding if it's really better.

Why Is This a Mistake?

Not everything new is better. Sometimes, old things work just as well! Judging something only by how new it is can make you miss out on other important details, like how useful or fun it really is.

Why Do People Do This?

- They think new means exciting and better.
- They like being the first to try something.
- They believe old things are always worse.

How to Avoid This Mistake

1. **Ask Questions:** Think, "Is this better, or just newer?"
2. **Test It Out:** Try new things, but don't forget to compare them to what you already know works.
3. **Don't Judge Too Quickly:** Give old things a chance before tossing them aside.

Practice Example

Let's try!

- Kid 1: "This new marker set must be better than the old one!"
- You: "Let's try it first and see if it works better."

How to Handle the Pro-Innovation Bias

If someone is overly excited about something new, you can say:

1. "New doesn't always mean better — let's check it out first."
2. "What makes it better than what we already have?"
3. "Trying new things is fun, but it's smart to see if it really works."

Remember This:

It's fun to explore new ideas and things, but don't forget to think about how they compare to what already works. Not everything shiny and new is better!

Chapter 44: The Halo Effect Fallacy

What Is It?

The Halo Effect happens when you think everything about a person or thing is amazing, just because one part of it is great. It's like saying, "She's good at soccer, so she must be good at math too!" But being awesome at one thing doesn't automatically make someone great at everything else.

Here's an Example:

- Kid 1: "This candy tastes amazing! I bet it's super healthy too."

- Kid 2: "Just because it tastes good doesn't mean it's good for you!"

See the mistake? Kid 1 assumes one good thing (the taste) makes everything about the candy good. But Kid 2 knows better.

Why Is This a Mistake?

When you let one good thing create a "halo," it can cloud your judgment. You might miss the not-so-great stuff, like candy being unhealthy or a good soccer player not being great at math. It's important to look at the whole picture, not just the shiny parts.

Why Do People Do This?

- They focus on the good stuff and ignore the bad.
- They want to believe something is perfect.
- It's easier to make a quick judgment than to think deeply.

How to Avoid This Mistake:

1. **Look Closer:** Ask yourself, "Is everything about this really amazing?"
2. **Separate the Parts:** Think about each part on its own instead of letting one good thing take over.
3. **Stay Curious:** Don't assume—ask questions to find the truth.

Practice Example

Let's try!

- Kid 1: "She's the best soccer player! I bet she's the smartest too."
- You: "Being good at soccer is great, but let's see how she does in other things first."

How to Handle the Halo Effect Fallacy

If someone is dazzled by one good thing, you can say:

1. "That part is awesome, but let's think about the other stuff too."
2. "What makes you think everything else is just as great?"
3. "It's okay to like something, but let's not ignore the facts."

Remember This:

One great thing doesn't make everything great. Keep your eyes open and think about the big picture. That way, you'll always make smarter choices!

Chapter 45: The Planning Fallacy

What Is It?

The Planning Fallacy happens when you think something will be faster or easier than it really is. It's like saying, "I'll clean my whole room in 10 minutes!" and then realizing it takes way longer because you keep finding toys to play with.

Here's an Example:

- Kid 1: "This art project will take me just an hour to finish!"
- Kid 2: "Are you sure? Don't forget you need time to draw, paint, and let it dry!"

What's going on? Kid 1 underestimates how much time the project will really take, but Kid 2 knows there's more to the task than it seems.

Why Is This a Mistake?

If you don't plan properly, you might run out of time or get overwhelmed. Big projects, like homework or cleaning, often have extra steps you don't think about at first.

Why Do People Do This?

- They focus on the easy parts and forget the tricky ones.
- They want to get started quickly without thinking it through.
- They feel excited and underestimate the effort needed.

How to Avoid This Mistake

1. **Break It Down:** Think about all the steps and how long each one will take.
2. **Add Extra Time:** Give yourself a little more time than you think you need.
3. **Ask for Help:** If you're not sure, ask someone who's done it before.

Practice Example

Let's try!

- Kid 1: "I can finish this puzzle before dinner!"
- You: "That's cool, but don't forget to count how many pieces there are!"

How to Handle the Planning Fallacy

If someone thinks a task will be quick and easy, you can say:

1. "Let's list out all the steps — it might take longer than you think."
2. "It's better to plan for more time than to run out!"
3. "Getting things done well is more important than rushing."

Remember This:

Good planning takes time! If you think through all the steps and give yourself extra time, you'll finish your tasks without stress—and maybe even have fun doing them.

Chapter 46: The Self-Sealing Fallacy

What Is It?

The Self-Sealing Fallacy happens when someone makes an argument that can't be proven wrong, no matter what. They keep changing the rules or the argument to make it impossible to disagree. It's like saying, "If I win, it's because I'm awesome, and if I lose, it's because the game was unfair!"

Here's an Example:

- Kid 1: "I'm the fastest runner!"
- Kid 2: "But I just beat you in a race."
- Kid 1: "That doesn't count because I wasn't trying my best!"

What's going on? Kid 1 keeps changing the rules to protect their argument. No matter what Kid 2 says, Kid 1 finds a way to stay "right."

Why Is This a Mistake?

Arguments like this can't be proven or tested because the person keeps shifting the goalposts. It's not fair, and it makes it hard to have a real conversation or figure out the truth.

Why Do People Do This?

- They don't want to admit they might be wrong.
- They think changing the argument makes them look smarter.
- They want to win at all costs.

How to Avoid This Mistake

1. **Stick to One Idea:** Make your point clear and don't keep changing it.
2. **Be Open to Feedback:** If someone challenges your argument, think about what they're saying.
3. **Respect the Rules:** Don't bend the argument just to stay right.

Practice Example

Let's try!

- Kid 1: "I'm great at drawing!"
- Kid 2: "But you didn't win the art contest."
- Kid 1: "That's because the judges don't know good art!"

How to Handle the Self-Sealing Fallacy

If someone keeps changing their argument, you can say:

1. "Can we agree on one idea and stick to it?"
2. "It's okay to be wrong sometimes — it helps us learn!"
3. "Let's focus on what we can both agree on."

Remember This:

Changing the rules to always be right isn't right. The best way to grow and learn is by listening to others and being honest about what's true!

Chapter 47: The Misleading Vividness Fallacy

What Is It?

The Misleading Vividness Fallacy happens when one dramatic example is used to make a point, even if it's not common or likely. It's like saying, "We shouldn't eat apples because one kid once choked on one!" That's scary, but it doesn't mean apples are bad for everyone.

Here's an Example:

- Kid 1: "Don't ride bikes —my cousin fell off and got hurt!"
- Kid 2: "That's sad, but lots of kids ride bikes safely every day."

Spotted the mistake? Kid 1 is using one scary story to argue against biking, but Kid 2 knows that one example doesn't tell the whole story.

Why Is This a Mistake?

Big, scary stories can stick in your head, but they don't always show what usually happens. If you focus on just one vivid example, you might ignore the facts or the bigger picture.

Why Do People Do This?

- Scary or exciting stories are easier to remember than boring facts.
- They want to grab attention and make their argument sound stronger.
- They don't realize one example isn't enough to prove a point.

How to Avoid This Mistake

1. **Look at the Bigger Picture:** Think about how often something actually happens.
2. **Check the Facts:** Don't rely on one example—find more information.
3. **Stay Calm:** Don't let scary stories make you forget the truth.

Practice Example

Let's try!

- Kid 1: "Don't go swimming — there was a shark attack on TV!"
- You: "Shark attacks are super rare. Let's learn how to swim safely instead."

How to Handle the Misleading Vividness Fallacy

If someone uses a dramatic example to make a point, you can say:

1. "That's one story, but does it happen a lot?"
2. "Let's see what the facts say about this."
3. "It's important to think about what usually happens, not just one time."

Remember This:

Exciting or scary stories can grab your attention, but they don't always show the full truth. Facts and patterns are better tools for making smart choices!

Chapter 48: The False Consensus Effect

What Is It?

The False Consensus Effect happens when someone thinks that most people agree with them, even if they don't. It's like saying, "Everyone loves pineapple on pizza because I do!" But wait — have they asked everyone?

Here's an Example:

- Kid 1: "Everyone at school agrees my team should win!"
- Kid 2: "Did you ask everyone, or just your friends?"

What's happening? Kid 1 assumes everyone thinks the same way they do, but Kid 2 knows that's not how opinions work.

Why Is This a Mistake?

It's easy to think your opinion is super popular because it feels right to you. But not everyone sees things the same way, and assuming they do can lead to bad decisions.

Why Do People Do This?

- They spend time with people who think like them, so it feels like "everyone" agrees.
- They don't stop to think that other people might have different ideas.
- It's easier to assume agreement than to ask for opinions.

How to Avoid This Mistake

1. **Ask Around:** Don't assume—find out what others actually think.
2. **Be Open to Differences:** Understand that not everyone sees things your way.
3. **Check the Facts:** Use evidence instead of guessing how popular an idea is.

Practice Example

Let's try!

- Kid 1: "Everyone loves this band—they're the best!"
- You: "I don't like them much. Maybe not *everyone* agrees with you!"

How to Handle the False Consensus Effect

If someone assumes everyone agrees with them, you can say:

1. "That's what you think, but have you asked other people?"
2. "Just because you like it doesn't mean everyone does."
3. "It's okay if people have different favorites — that's what makes things fun!"

Remember This:

Not everyone sees the world the same way, and that's okay! It's important to listen and learn from others instead of assuming everyone agrees with you.

Chapter 49: The Argument from Repetition (Ad Nauseam) Fallacy

What Is It?

The Argument from Repetition happens when someone repeats an idea over and over to make it seem true. It's like saying, "If I say it enough, everyone will believe me!" But repeating something doesn't make it right.

Here's an Example:

- Kid 1: "I'm the best at basketball!"
- Kid 2: "You've said that a hundred times, but you still miss most of your shots!"

What's going on? Kid 1 keeps repeating their claim, but Kid 2 knows that saying it over and over doesn't make it true.

Why Is This a Mistake?

Repetition can make an idea feel more familiar, but it doesn't prove it's right. A good argument needs facts, not just lots of talking.

Why Do People Do This?

- They think saying something enough will make people believe it.
- They don't have strong facts, so they rely on repetition.
- They hope others will stop questioning them if they hear it often.

How to Avoid This Mistake

1. **Use Facts, Not Repetition:** Share evidence, not just the same words.
2. **Listen to Others:** Don't keep repeating—hear what they have to say.
3. **Stay Open-Minded:** Be ready to change your mind if the facts don't match.

Practice Example:

Let's try!

- Kid 1: "This toy is the coolest! This toy is the coolest!"
- You: "Why do you think it's the coolest? Can you explain?"

How to Handle the Argument from Repetition:

If someone keeps repeating themselves, you can say:

1. "You've said that already — what's your reason?"
2. "Repeating doesn't make it true—can we look at the facts?"
3. "Let's talk about why you think that instead of just saying it again."

Remember This:

Saying something over and over doesn't make it true. Good arguments need strong evidence, not just lots of words!

Chapter 50: Poisoning the Well

What Is It?

Poisoning the Well happens when someone tries to make you dislike or mistrust someone else's argument before you even hear it. It's like saying, "Don't listen to her — she doesn't know anything!" before she's even had a chance to speak. This fallacy is like putting a big "Don't trust this person!" sign in front of someone, which isn't fair at all.

Here's an Example:

- Kid 1: "Don't listen to Sam — he never tells the truth!"
- Sam: "Hey, that's not true! You haven't even heard what I have to say yet!"

What's happening here? Kid 1 is trying to make everyone doubt Sam before Sam has even started talking. That's Poisoning the Well! It distracts people from the actual idea and focuses on making someone look bad instead.

Why Is This a Mistake?

This is a mistake because it's unfair to judge someone's ideas before hearing them out. Imagine if someone said nobody should listen to your idea just because they don't like you—that wouldn't feel good, would it? By dismissing someone before they get a chance to speak, we might miss out on something smart or helpful.

Why Do People Do This?

- **They're scared of losing the argument:** If the other person has a good point, they try to stop others from listening to it.
- **It's easier than explaining their own ideas:** They'd rather attack the person than focus on the argument.
- **They want to control the conversation:** By making others look bad, they hope people will only listen to them.

How to Avoid This Mistake

1. **Listen first:** Always hear what someone has to say before deciding if it's good or bad.
2. **Talk about ideas, not people:** Focus on the message, not who's delivering it.
3. **Stay open-minded:** Give everyone a fair chance to share their thoughts without pre-judging.

Practice Example

Let's try!

- Kid 1: "Don't listen to Emma — she's always wrong!"
- You: "Let's hear what Emma has to say first. Everyone deserves a chance."

How to Handle Poisoning the Well

If someone tries to dismiss an idea before you've even heard it, here's what you can do:

1. **Stay neutral:** "Let's be fair and listen before we decide."
2. **Point out the unfairness:** "It's not right to judge without hearing their idea."
3. **Encourage fairness:** "I'd like to hear both sides before making up my mind."

Remember This:

Judging someone before they speak is like closing a book before reading the first page. You might miss out on something amazing! Ideas should be judged on what they are, not who they come from. Give everyone a fair chance, and you'll always be closer to the truth.

Conclusion: Thinking Clearly in a World of Silly Arguments!

Congratulations, logical thinker! You've just completed a big journey through the world of tricky arguments and sneaky fallacies. Now, you're ready to use your new superpower — clear thinking!

The world is full of people trying to persuade you of all sorts of things. Some will be fair, and others might try to confuse you. But don't worry — you've got the tools to spot silly arguments, ask smart questions, and focus on what really matters.

Always remember:

- **Be Curious:** Ask questions and dig deeper. The truth loves a curious mind!

- **Be Fair:** Listen to others and consider their ideas, even if you don't agree at first.

- **Be Brave:** Don't be afraid to say, "Wait a second, that doesn't make sense!" when something feels off.

You're now a champion of clear thinking, ready to handle tricky debates, tricky ideas, and even your everyday conversations. The world needs more people like you—people who think with their heads and their hearts. So, go ahead, use your skills, and make smarter decisions. You're ready to shine!

Appendix A: Quick Reference Guide to Logical Fallacies

Use this list for a quick reminder of each fallacy. This quick guide makes it easy to recall and detect fallacies anytime!

1. **Ad Hominem:** Attacking the person instead of the idea.

   "You're wrong because you're too young!"

2. **Straw Man:** Misrepresenting someone's argument to make it easier to attack.

   "You want us to never eat candy again? That's too extreme!"

3. **False Dilemma:** Pretending there are only two choices when there are more.

   "It's my way or the highway!"

4. **Bandwagon:** Believing something is true because everyone else does.

   "Everyone says this game is the best, so it must be true!"

5. **Appeal to Authority:** Assuming something is true just because an expert says so.

   "The CEO said it's great, so it must be!"

6. **Appeal to Emotion:** Using feelings instead of facts to persuade.

   "If you don't agree, you'll make everyone sad!"

7. **Hasty Generalization:** Jumping to a conclusion without enough evidence.

   "All cats are mean because my cat scratched me!"

8. **Slippery Slope:** Saying one small thing will lead to a big disaster.

   "If we allow one cookie before dinner, we'll eat junk food forever!"

9. **Red Herring:** Distracting from the topic with something unrelated.

   "We're talking about homework, not my messy room!"

10. **Circular Reasoning:** Using the conclusion as proof of itself.

    "I'm right because I said so!"

11. **Loaded Question:** Asking a question that traps the other person.

    "Why are you always so lazy?"

12. **Gambler's Fallacy:** Believing past events affect future outcomes.

    "This coin has landed on heads three times—it's due for tails!"

13. **Appeal to Tradition:** Thinking something is right because it's old or traditional.

    "We've always done it this way, so it must be best!"

14. **Sunk Cost Fallacy:** Sticking with something because you've already invested in it.

    "I can't quit now—I've already spent so much time on it!"

15. **Middle Ground:** Assuming the truth is somewhere between two extremes.

    "Maybe the Earth is kind of round and kind of flat."

16. **Cherry Picking:** Only using the facts that support your argument.

    "Look! This one piece of data proves I'm right!"

17. **Appeal to Nature:** Believing something is better because it's natural.

    "This snack is natural, so it must be healthy!"

18. **Appeal to Consequences:** Judging something as true or false based on its effects.

    "If this is true, it would be bad—so it can't be true!"

19. **Personal Incredulity:** Thinking something isn't true because it's hard to understand.

"I don't get how this works, so it must be fake!"

20. **Appeal to Novelty:** Believing something is better because it's new.

"This gadget is new, so it's the best!"

21. **No True Scotsman:** Changing the rules of a group to exclude someone.

"No real soccer fan would like that team!"

22. **Texas Sharpshooter:** Only focusing on information that supports your argument.

"These three wins prove I'm the best!"

23. **Survivorship Bias:** Ignoring the failures and only looking at successes.

"If they made it big, so can anyone!"

24. **Scare Tactic:** Using fear to win an argument instead of facts.

"If you don't agree, something terrible will happen!"

25. **Appeal to Personal Experience:** Thinking your own story proves everything.

"I've seen it happen, so it must be true for everyone!"

26. **Composition Fallacy:** Assuming the whole is good because the parts are good.

"All these puzzle pieces look great, so the picture must be amazing!"

27. **Division Fallacy:** Assuming every part is true because the whole is true.

"This cake is delicious, so every ingredient must taste good!"

28. **Appeal to Hypocrisy:** Dodging the argument by pointing out someone else's flaws.

"You can't tell me to clean up—you're messy too!"

29. **Appeal to Pity:** Using sympathy to win instead of evidence.

"You should let me go first because I had a bad day."

30. **False Equivalence:** Treating two unequal things as if they're the same.

"Cats and fish are the same—they're both pets!"

31. **Genetic Fallacy:** Judging something based on where it came from.

"That idea came from him, so it must be bad."

32. **Argument from Silence:** Thinking no evidence means something isn't true.

"If no one said it, it must not be real."

33. **Appeal to Probability:** Believing something will happen just because it could.

"It's possible, so it's definitely going to happen!"

34. **Fallacy of Relative Privation:** Saying one problem isn't important because there's a bigger problem.

"Why care about your broken toy? Some kids have no toys!"

35. **Appeal to Force:** Using threats instead of reasons to persuade.

"You'd better agree, or else!"

36. **Appeal to Flattery:** Using compliments to win someone over.

"You're so smart—don't you agree with me?"

37. **False Attribution:** Believing something is true just because an unreliable source said so.

"A random website said it, so it must be true!"

38. **Broken Window Fallacy:** Thinking damage is good because it creates jobs to fix it.

"Breaking stuff helps the economy!"

39. **Appeal to Common Sense:** Saying something must be true because it seems obvious.

"It's common sense—why question it?"

40. **False Balance:** Treating two sides as equal even when one has better evidence.

"Let's give both opinions the same weight, even if one is weaker."

41. **Just-World Fallacy:** Believing the world is always fair.

"If something bad happened, they must have deserved it."

42. **Ludic Fallacy:** Assuming real life works like a game or simulation.

"I won this video game, so I can do the same in real life!"

43. **Pro-Innovation Bias:** Thinking new things are always better.

"This new gadget must be the best!"

44. **Halo Effect:** Letting one good trait influence your judgment on everything else.

"They're good at art, so they must be great at math too!"

45. **Planning Fallacy:** Underestimating how long something will take.

"We'll finish this project in one hour—easy!"

46. **Self-Sealing Fallacy:** Making an argument impossible to prove wrong.

"If you don't agree, you just don't understand!"

47. **Misleading Vividness:** Using one dramatic example to make a big claim.

"That one accident proves flying is unsafe!"

48. **False Consensus Effect:** Believing everyone thinks the same as you.

"Everyone loves this book—it's the best!"

49. **Argument from Repetition:** Thinking something is true just because it's repeated.

"I've told you this ten times, so it must be true!"

50. **Poisoning the Well:** Discrediting someone before they even speak.

"Don't listen to them—they're always wrong!"

Appendix B: Practice Scenarios for Kids (Spot the Fallacy Game!)

Below are 15 fun and engaging scenarios for you to figure out which fallacy is being used. Read each one carefully, and then check the answers at the end of this section to see if you're a fallacy detective!

1. The Movie Star Expert

Kid 1: "This toothpaste is the best because a famous actor said so!"

Kid 2: "What does acting have to do with toothpaste?"

What's the fallacy?

2. The Mean Math Teacher

Kid 1: "Our math teacher says 2+2=4, but they're so strict! They can't be right."

Kid 2: "But does their personality change the math?"

What's the fallacy?

3. The Ultimate Toy Debate

Kid 1: "Either you like this toy, or you don't like fun at all!"

Kid 2: "Wait, can't I like other toys too?"

What's the fallacy?

4. The Popular Choice

Kid 1: "Everyone is wearing these shoes, so they must be the best!"

Kid 2: "Does popularity always mean quality?"

What's the fallacy?

5. The Candy Catastrophe

Kid 1: "If you eat one candy, you'll end up eating ten and get cavities!"

Kid 2: "That seems like a big leap."

What's the fallacy?

6. The Tricky Question

Kid 1: "Why do you always forget to do your chores?"

Kid 2: "Wait, who said I always forget?"

What's the fallacy?

7. The Fancy Professor

Kid 1: "This professor said the moon is made of cheese, so it must be true!"

Kid 2: "Do they have proof for that?"

What's the fallacy?

8. The "Real Fan" Rule

Kid 1: "If you don't watch every game, you're not a real fan of the team."

Kid 2: "Can't I be a fan and miss some games?"

What's the fallacy?

9. The Fear Tactic

Kid 1: "If you don't do your homework, the teacher will yell at you forever!"

Kid 2: "That's a bit extreme."

What's the fallacy?

10. The Puzzle Problem

Kid 1: "All these puzzle pieces are colorful, so the final picture must be beautiful!"

Kid 2: "What if the picture doesn't make sense, even if the pieces are pretty?"

What's the fallacy?

---

11. The Amazing Athlete

Kid 1: "She's so good at sports, so she must be the best person to help us with math homework!"

Kid 2: "What does sports have to do with math?"

What's the fallacy?

---

12. The Weather Expert

Kid 1: "It hasn't rained all week, so it definitely won't rain tomorrow."

Kid 2: "Is that how weather works?"

What's the fallacy?

---

13. The Big Problem Argument

Kid 1: "Why are you worried about your missing notebook? Some people don't even have school supplies."

Kid 2: "Can't both be problems?"

What's the fallacy?

---

14. The Repeating Rule

Kid 1: "I've told you five times that I'm right, so I must be!"

Kid 2: "Saying it more doesn't make it true."

What's the fallacy?

---

15. The Garden Argument

Kid 1: "Plants are natural, so they're always good for you."

Kid 2: "What about poison ivy?"

What's the fallacy?

Answers: Spot the Fallacy

1. Appeal to Authority
2. Ad Hominem
3. False Dilemma
4. Bandwagon
5. Slippery Slope
6. Loaded Question
7. Appeal to Authority
8. No True Scotsman
9. Scare Tactic
10. Composition Fallacy
11. Halo Effect
12. Appeal to Probability
13. Fallacy of Relative Privation
14. Argument from Repetition
15. Appeal to Nature

Have fun spotting these fallacies in real life and practice keeping your thinking sharp!

Appendix C: Tips for Debating and Winning Arguments

Debating can be fun and a great way to learn new things. Whether you're talking with your friends, classmates, or even adults, it's important to stay calm, listen carefully, and use good reasoning. Here are some tips to help you debate like a pro and win arguments the smart way:

1. Stay Cool, Stay Kind

- Don't get angry or mean, even if the other person does. People listen better when you stay calm and friendly.
- Remember, winning an argument doesn't mean making someone feel bad — it's about helping them see the truth.

2. Listen Like a Detective

- Pay attention to what the other person says. Are they making any fallacies or mistakes in their argument?
- Ask questions to understand their point of view better, like, "Can you explain why you think that?"

3. Use Facts, Not Feelings

- Base your argument on evidence, research, and logic—not just opinions or emotions.
- Example: Instead of saying, "I feel this is right," say, "Here's why this works: [insert facts]."

4. Ask Good Questions

- Challenge ideas politely by asking questions like:
  - "What's your evidence for that?"
  - "What if things work differently than you think?"

- Questions help others think more clearly and find flaws in their argument.

5. Spot the Fallacies

- Watch out for common mistakes like:
    - "Everyone says it, so it must be true!" (Bandwagon Fallacy)
    - "This is just common sense!" (Appeal to Common Sense Fallacy)
- Politely point out these errors to make your case stronger.

6. Keep It Simple

- Use clear, simple words to explain your point. Don't confuse others with complicated language or too many ideas at once.
- Example: Instead of saying, "This hypothesis is flawed," say, "That idea has some problems."

7. Know When to Stop

- If the other person refuses to listen or keeps getting upset, it's okay to end the debate. You can say, "Let's agree to disagree for now."
- Sometimes, it's better to walk away than to argue forever.

8. Be Open to Learning

- If someone makes a good point, don't be afraid to admit it. Saying, "You're right about that," shows you're fair and willing to learn.
- A good debate isn't about "winning" but finding the truth together.

9. Practice, Practice, Practice

- Try debating with your friends or family on fun topics, like "What's the best pizza topping?" or "Should kids have more recess?"
- The more you practice, the better you'll get at spotting fallacies and explaining your ideas clearly.

10. Stay Curious

- Always be ready to learn something new. Read books, ask questions, and stay curious about the world. The more you know, the stronger your arguments will be!

Final Thought

Debating is like a fun game for your brain. You get to practice thinking, listening, and learning. Even if you don't "win" every argument, you'll grow smarter and more confident every time you try. So keep talking, keep learning, and keep thinking clearly — you've got this!

Part 2: Decision-Making for Kids

The Illustrated Guide to Choosing Wisely, Avoiding Mistakes, and Knowing What to Do!

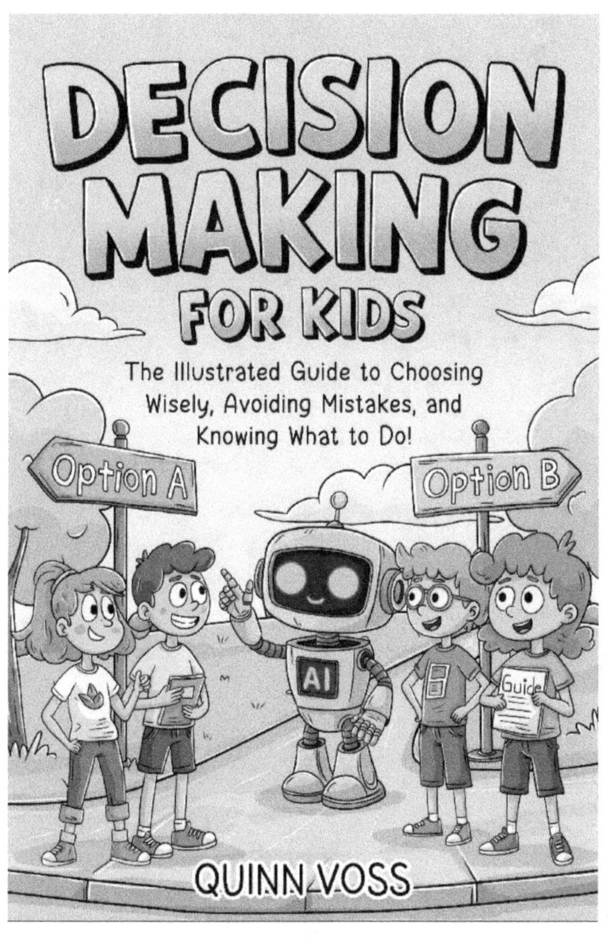

Introduction
Welcome to the world of decision-making! Why learning to make good choices makes you smarter

Hey there! Did you know that every day, you make **hundreds** of decisions? From what to eat for breakfast to what game to play, your brain is *always* making choices.

But here's the big question: **Are you making the BEST choices?**

What Makes a Good Decision?

A good decision is like picking the right path in a maze. Some paths lead to treasure (yay!), while others lead to dead ends (uh-oh!). When you make a smart choice, things work out better. When you make a rushed or bad choice, well... you might end up wishing you had thought it through!

Here's an example:

- Imagine you're at a store, and you see a **cool new toy.** You REALLY want it.
- But wait! If you spend your money now, you **won't** have enough for that awesome game you were saving for.
- What do you do? Buy the toy now or wait for the game?

This is where **smart decision-making** helps! Instead of just acting on what you *want* right now, you think ahead.

Making great choices can:

- **Save you from mistakes** – No more "I wish I hadn't done that" moments.
- **Help you get what you really want** – Instead of wasting time or money, you make choices that pay off.
- **Make life easier** – When you know how to make smart decisions, you feel more confident and in control.

How This Book Works

This book will teach you the secrets of **smart decision-making!** You'll learn:

- How to avoid common thinking mistakes (your brain can be sneaky!).
- Simple tricks to help you choose wisely.
- Fun ways to test your decision-making skills!

By the time you're done, you'll be a **decision-making pro** — ready to tackle any choice that comes your way!

So, let's jump in and start **choosing wisely!**

SECTION I
What Makes a Good Decision?

Every day, you make choices—what to eat, what to play, who to talk to. But **how do you know if you're making the best choice?** A good decision isn't just about what feels right *now* — it's about thinking ahead and choosing what's best for **you and your future.** In this section, you'll learn **how your brain makes decisions, what tricks it plays on you, and how to spot bad choices before they happen!**

Chapter 1: The Science of Choice – How We Make Decisions

Every day, you make decisions—what to eat, what to wear, what to play. But have you ever wondered *how* you make those choices?

Let's say you're picking a snack. You see a **chocolate bar** and an **apple**. Which one do you choose?

At first, it seems simple. But inside your brain, two different parts are working:

1. **Fast Thinking** – "Chocolate! It's sweet and delicious! Grab it now!"

2. **Slow Thinking** – "Wait ... an apple is healthier and will give me energy. Maybe that's the better choice."

This happens all the time. Sometimes, your brain makes quick choices without thinking too hard. Other times, it slows down and carefully weighs the options.

Why Quick Choices Aren't Always Smart

Long ago, humans needed to make fast decisions to survive. If they saw a wild animal, they didn't stop to think—they *ran!* That fast-thinking instinct is still in your brain today.

But now, most decisions aren't life or death. Instead, they involve **long-term effects** — like saving money, making friends, or choosing to study instead of playing video games.

That's when slow thinking becomes important. **It helps you make smarter choices by thinking ahead.**

The Secret to Better Decisions

Next time you're making a choice, try this:

1. **Pause** – Give yourself a moment to think.
2. **Ask** – "What will happen if I choose this?"
3. **Decide** – Pick the choice that helps you in the long run.

The more you practice, the better your choices will be. And to make even *smarter* decisions, you need to understand the battle between **logic and emotion**—which we'll talk about next!

Chapter 2: Logic vs. Emotion – Thinking vs. Feeling

Imagine you're at a store and see a **new toy** you really want. You have money, but you were saving up for a **bigger toy** later.

Now, two voices start arguing in your head:

- **Your Feelings Say:** "Buy it now! It looks awesome! You'll have fun today!"
- **Your Thinking Brain Says:** "But wait ... if you buy this, you won't have enough for the bigger toy later."

This is the battle between **emotion (feelings)** and **logic (thinking)**.

When Emotion Takes Over

Feelings help us enjoy life, but they can also push us into **bad choices**. That's why people sometimes:

- Stay up late watching TV, even though they'll be tired the next day.
- Eat too much candy, even though they'll get a stomach-ache.

- Buy something impulsively, even though they were saving for something better.

When Logic Takes Over

Logic helps us make smart decisions, but if we **only** use logic, life might feel boring or strict. Imagine if:

- You never ate dessert because it wasn't "necessary."
- You never did anything fun because it wasn't "productive."
- You only made choices based on facts and ignored how you felt.

That wouldn't be fun either! The key is to **balance both**.

How to Balance Logic and Emotion

Next time you have a big decision, try this trick:

1. **Ask two questions:**
   - What do my feelings say?
   - What does my thinking brain say?
2. **Pause and compare both answers.**
3. **Make a choice that makes sense but also feels right.**

The best choices come when **logic and emotion work together.** Now, let's learn some tricks to avoid **thinking mistakes** that can lead to bad decisions!

Chapter 3: The Decision-Making Blueprint – Steps to a Smart Choice

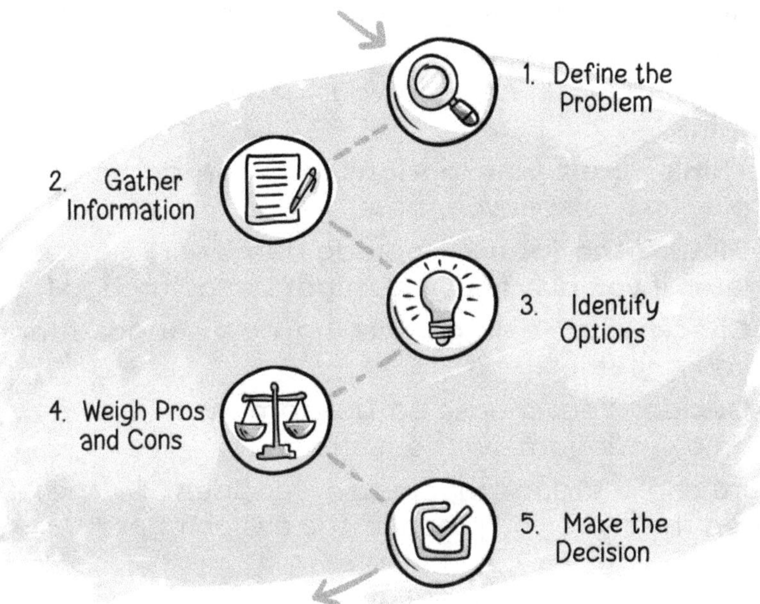

Some decisions are easy — like picking what socks to wear. But others? Not so simple! **Should you join the soccer team or the art club? Should you spend or save your money?** Big choices can feel tricky, but don't worry! There's a simple **blueprint** to help you make **smart decisions every time.**

The 5 Steps to a Smart Choice

1. **Pause.** Instead of deciding *right away*, stop for a moment. Rushed choices often lead to mistakes!

2. **Think about your options.** What choices do you have? List them out. Sometimes, there's more than just "yes" or "no."

3. **Picture the future.** What will happen if you choose each option? Think ahead! Will this choice help you tomorrow, next week, or next year?

4. **Check your feelings.** Are you making this choice just because it feels good **right now**? Or does it also make sense for the future?

5. **Decide and move forward.** Once you've thought it through, **pick the best choice and go with it!**

Let's Practice!

Imagine you're deciding whether to do your homework now or play first.

1. **Pause.** Don't just grab your game controller—stop and think!

2. **Think about your options.** You can do homework first, play first, or split your time.

3. **Picture the future.** If you do homework now, you'll relax later. If you play first, you might be too tired to focus.

4. **Check your feelings.** Playing now sounds fun, but will you regret it later?

5. **Decide.** You choose to do homework first so you can enjoy your game without stress!

Smart choices don't happen by accident — they follow a **plan.** And the more you practice, the easier it gets!

Chapter 4: The Role of Bias – What Tricks Your Brain?

Your brain is amazing—it helps you solve problems, learn new things, and make decisions. But guess what? **Sometimes, your brain plays tricks on you!** These thinking mistakes are called **biases**, and they can lead to **bad decisions** if you don't catch them.

3 Common Biases That Trick You

The First Answer Bias – Your brain likes to **stick with the first thing you hear**, even if it's wrong.

Example: Your friend tells you a new kid is "mean," so you believe it without talking to them yourself.

The "Everyone Else Is Doing It" Bias – Your brain thinks that if others are doing something, it must be a good idea.

Example: Your friends are skipping practice, so you feel like skipping too—even though you know it's a bad choice.

The "It's Always Been This Way" Bias – Your brain assumes that just because something **worked before,** it must be the best choice now.

Example: You always pick the same meal at your favorite restaurant, even though there might be something better!

How to Outsmart These Tricks

- **Stop and Question It** – "Wait… am I choosing this just because it's the first thing I heard?"
- **Think for Yourself** – Just because others do it doesn't mean it's the best choice.
- **Try Something New** – Be open to different ideas instead of doing things the same way every time.

Biases **aren't** bad—they're just shortcuts your brain uses. But if you don't notice them, they can **lead you the wrong way.** And that's why awareness is so important!

Chapter 5: The Power of Awareness – Noticing When You're About to Make a Bad Choice

Have you ever done something and **immediately regretted it**? Maybe you said something mean without thinking, or you picked the wrong answer on a test because you rushed. Afterward, you might have thought, *Why did I do that?*

The answer is simple: **You weren't aware in the moment.**

Awareness is like having a **pause button** for your brain. When you're aware, you can **catch bad decisions before they happen.** But when you're not paying attention, you might make choices you wish you could take back.

How Do People Make Bad Choices?

People usually make bad choices when they act **too fast**, don't think about the future, or let their emotions take over. Here are some common traps:

- **Acting Without Thinking** – You blurt out an answer in class without double-checking, and it turns out to be wrong.

- **Giving In to Pressure** – Your friends want to skip practice, so you join them, even though you know you shouldn't.

- **Letting Feelings Take Over** – You're upset and slam a door, then realize you made things worse.

Bad choices don't just happen. **There are warning signs — if you know where to look.**

Signs You Might Be About to Make a Bad Choice

1. **You feel rushed.** Quick decisions often lead to mistakes. If you feel like you're deciding *too fast*, stop and take a breath.

2. **You feel pressured.** If the only reason you're doing something is because *everyone else is*, that's a sign to pause and think.

3. **You're ignoring that little voice in your head.** If something feels *off*, it probably is. Pay attention to that feeling.

4. **You're only thinking about right now.** Ask yourself, *Will this decision still seem like a good idea tomorrow?* If the answer is no, rethink it.

How to Stay Aware and Make Better Choices

Being aware of your thoughts and actions takes practice, but here are three simple tricks that help:

1. **Use the "Pause and Picture" Rule** – Before making a decision, stop and picture what might happen next. If it looks like trouble, change your choice.

2. **Ask Yourself One Simple Question** – *Will I be happy with this decision later?* If you think you might regret it, take a step back.

3. **Listen to Your Gut Feeling** – If something feels wrong, even if you can't explain why, it's worth taking a second to think before acting.

Imagine you're in class, and your friend whispers the answer to a question. You *know* you shouldn't cheat, but you really want to get it right. Before you decide, you:

- **Pause.** Instead of answering right away, you stop and think.
- **Picture the future.** If you cheat, you might get caught. Even if you don't, will you really feel proud of that grade?
- **Check your feelings.** Your gut tells you this isn't the right thing to do.

You decide to answer on your own—even if you get it wrong, at least it's honest. **That's the power of awareness!**

The Secret to Catching Bad Choices Before They Happen

Making smart choices isn't just about *what* you decide—it's about *noticing* when you're about to make a mistake. The next time you feel rushed, pressured, or unsure, **pause and think.** The best decisions happen when you give yourself the chance to make them.

SECTION II
Super Smart Thinking Tricks

Great decision-makers don't just rely on guesses or feelings—they use smart thinking tricks to **break down problems, see things clearly, and make the best choice.** These simple strategies help you think **faster, smarter, and more creatively** so you can solve problems like a pro. In this section, you'll learn some of the best thinking tools, starting with **First Principles Thinking—one of the smartest ways to solve tough problems!**

Chapter 6: First Principles Thinking – Breaking Problems into Tiny Pieces

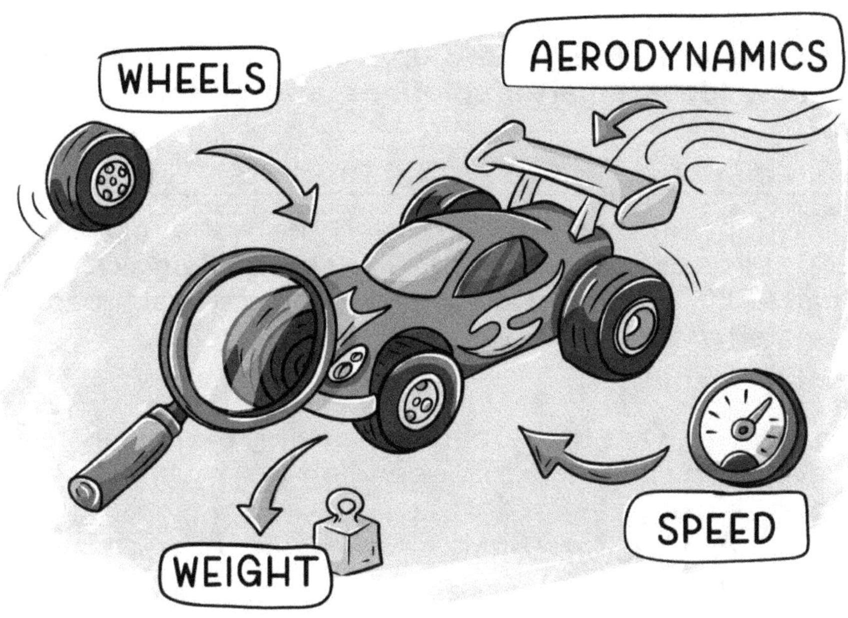

Imagine you're trying to build the **fastest toy car ever.** You could just grab the **biggest, shiniest** car at the store … or you could take it apart and **figure out what really makes a car fast.**

First Principles Thinking is about **breaking things down to their smallest parts** and building up from there. Instead of copying what already exists, you ask, *What do I actually need to solve this problem?*

How It Works

Most people solve problems by **doing what's always been done.** But First Principles Thinking helps you find **new and better solutions** by asking three key questions:

1. **What is the problem I need to solve?** (Example: I want to build a faster toy car.)

2. **What are the basic parts of this problem?** (Wheels, weight, aerodynamics, speed.)

3. **How can I improve each part to make the best solution?** (Lighter materials, smoother wheels, better design.)

Why This Works

Instead of just copying what's already out there, **you rebuild the solution from the ground up.** People who think this way invent **new ideas, smarter solutions, and better ways to do things!**

Real-Life Example: The Wright Brothers

The Wright Brothers, who invented the first airplane, didn't just copy birds or hot-air balloons. They **broke flying down into tiny parts**—lift, control, and speed—and tested each part until they created a working airplane!

Try It Yourself!

Let's say you want to get better at **saving money.** Instead of just saying, *"I need to stop spending so much,"* use First Principles Thinking:

- **Break it down.** Where is my money going? Snacks? Toys? Games?
- **Find new solutions.** Can I pack a snack instead of buying one? Can I trade games instead of buying new ones?
- **Test and improve.** Try your ideas, see what works, and adjust!

The Secret to Smarter Problem-Solving

First Principles Thinking **helps you invent new ideas, solve problems better, and make smarter choices.** Instead of guessing or copying what others do, break things down, rebuild them, and find the **best** way forward.

Chapter 7: Occam's Razor – The Easiest Answer is Often the Best

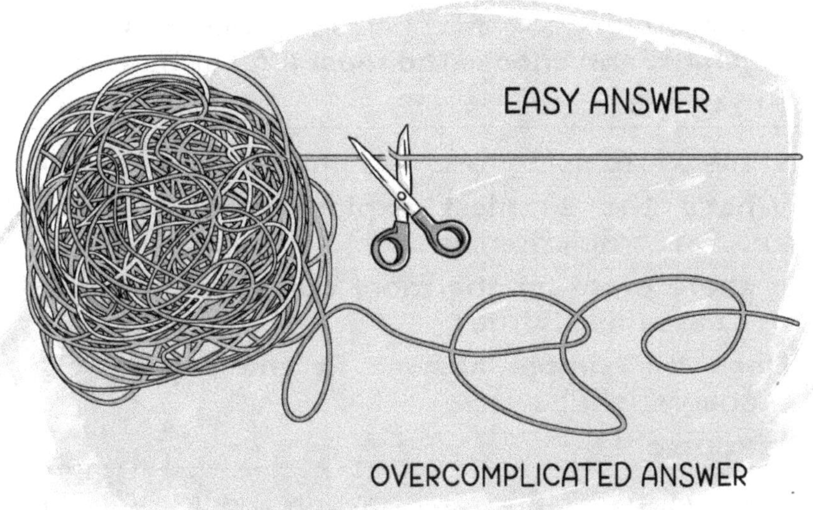

Imagine you wake up and see your bike is missing from the yard. What happened?

You come up with two ideas:

1. **A sneaky group of expert bike thieves used high-tech tools to steal it in the middle of the night.**

2. **You forgot to put it in the garage, and someone simply took it.**

Which one seems more likely?

Occam's Razor is a thinking trick that says: **The simplest explanation is usually the right one.** Instead of overcomplicating things, it helps you focus on the answer that makes the most sense.

Why Do People Ignore the Simple Answer?

People love exciting stories. If something goes wrong, the brain wants to come up with **big, dramatic reasons**—even when the real answer is simple.

For example:

- You text your friend, and they don't reply. Your brain **could** think: *They're mad at me! Maybe I did something wrong!*
- Or ... they just left their phone at home.

Instead of jumping to wild conclusions, **Occam's Razor helps you stop, think, and choose the most logical answer.**

How to Use Occam's Razor

Next time you're trying to solve a problem, ask yourself:

1. **What's the simplest explanation?** (Not everything needs a complicated answer.)
2. **Is there proof for the more complicated idea?** (If not, don't assume it's true.)
3. **Does the simple answer fit the facts?** (If yes, it's probably right!)

Try It Yourself!

Let's say you can't find your favorite book. Which is more likely?

- **Theory 1:** A secret book thief snuck in and took it.
- **Theory 2:** You left it in your backpack.

Occam's Razor reminds you to check your backpack first—because **most of the time, the easiest answer is the right one.**

The Secret to Thinking Clearly

When something happens, don't jump to wild conclusions. **Look for the simplest explanation first.** It will save you time, worry, and a lot of unnecessary confusion!

Chapter 8: The Pareto Principle – The 80/20 Rule of Smart Choices

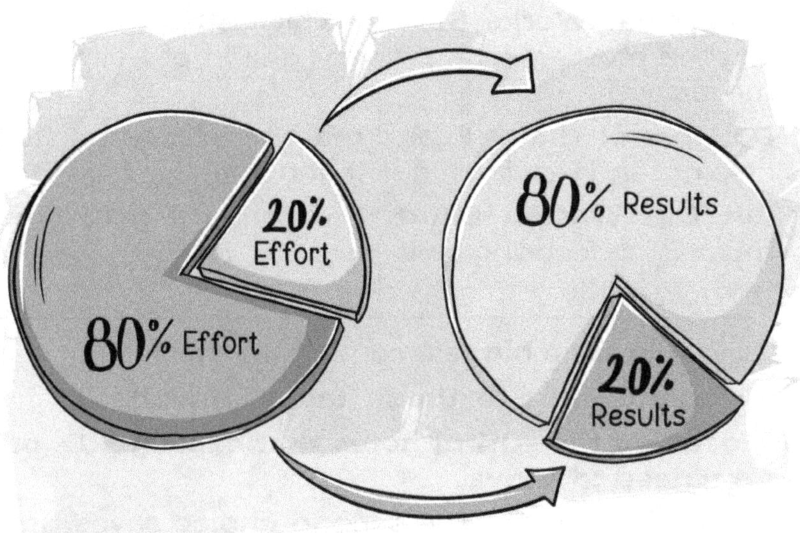

Imagine you have **10 toys,** but you only play with **2 of them** all the time. Or you have **a huge pile of clothes,** but you mostly wear the **same few favorites.**

That's the **Pareto Principle,** also called the **80/20 Rule**—it means that in many situations, **a small amount of effort or things create most of the results.**

How the 80/20 Rule Works

The Pareto Principle says that **about 80% of what happens comes from just 20% of the effort.**

Here are some examples:

- **In school:** You might learn **80% of a subject** from **20% of the lessons** that explain it best.
- **In sports: 20% of your practice drills** make you **80% better.**
- **In video games: 20% of your best strategies** help you win **80% of the time.**

The key to **working smarter, not harder** is figuring out

which 20% makes the biggest difference.

How to Use the Pareto Principle

Instead of trying to **do everything**, focus on the **small actions that give you the biggest results.**

1. **Find What Works Best.** – Which study method helps you the most? Which practice drill improves your game the fastest?
2. **Do More of That.** – Spend more time on what's actually helping, and less on things that don't.
3. **Cut Out Wasted Effort.** – If something isn't helping much, stop focusing on it.

Try It Yourself!

Let's say you have **a big test** coming up. You could:

- **Read the entire textbook (takes forever).**
- **Focus on the 20% of notes that explain 80% of what you need to know.**

Which one is smarter? **The second choice saves time and still helps you succeed.**

The Secret to Working Smarter

The Pareto Principle helps you **find what matters most and focus on it.** Instead of working harder on everything, **find the small things that make the biggest impact — and do more of those!**

Chapter 9: Second-Order Thinking – Thinking Ahead Before You Act

Imagine you're given a choice: **Would you rather eat a giant bowl of ice cream or a plate of vegetables?**

Your first thought might be, **"Ice cream! It's sweet and delicious!"** But what happens next? If you eat too much, you might get a stomach-ache. If you eat veggies, you'll feel strong and energized later.

This is where **Second-Order Thinking** comes in. Instead of only thinking about **what happens now**, it helps you think about **what happens next—and after that.**

First-Order vs. Second-Order Thinking

Most people stop at **first-order thinking**, which is only about what happens *right away.* But **second-order thinking** asks, *"And then what?"*

Let's look at an example:

- **First-Order Thinking:** "I'll stay up late to play video games because it's fun."

- **Second-Order Thinking:** "And then what? I'll be tired tomorrow. I won't focus in class. Maybe I should sleep instead."

The second-order thinker **sees the future effects of their choices.**

Why It's Important

People who only think about **right now** often make **bad decisions** because they don't see the bigger picture. Second-Order Thinking helps you:

- Avoid **regret** (so you don't think, *Why did I do that?*)
- Plan **smarter** (so you make choices that help you later).
- Outthink problems before they happen.

How to Use Second-Order Thinking

Next time you make a choice, ask yourself:

1. **What happens next?** (*If I do this, what's the immediate result?*)
2. **And then what?** (*What will happen later because of this?*)
3. **Is that what I really want?** (*Will this choice help me in the long run?*)

Try It Yourself!

You're about to **spend all your money on candy.** Stop and think:

- **First-Order Thinking:** "I get candy, and it tastes great!"
- **Second-Order Thinking:** "And then what? My money is gone. I won't be able to buy the cool thing I was saving for."

Now you can make a **smarter choice!**

Second-Order Thinking helps you **see the future effects of your choices.** Instead of only thinking about *right now*, ask yourself, *"And then what?"* This one simple question can help you make **better decisions every day.**

Chapter 10: Opportunity Cost – Picking One Thing Means Losing Another

Imagine you have **one movie ticket** and two choices:

1. Watch a fun action movie with your best friend.
2. Watch a cool science movie that teaches you something new.

You can only pick **one**. No matter what you choose, **you're also giving something up.** That's called **Opportunity Cost**—whenever you pick one thing, you're losing the chance to do something else.

What Is Opportunity Cost?

Opportunity Cost is **the hidden cost of every decision**. It's not about money—it's about what you *could have* done instead.

- If you **spend your allowance on a toy**, the cost is **not being able to buy something later**.
- If you **watch TV all afternoon**, the cost is **losing time to do homework or play outside**.

- If you **eat all your snacks today**, the cost is **not having any for tomorrow**.

Why It Matters

Many people don't think about **what they're losing** when they make a choice. But smart decision-makers **always consider the trade-offs.**

- Before spending money, ask: *Is this the best way to use it?*
- Before using time, ask: *Will I regret not doing something else?*
- Before saying yes to something, ask: *What am I saying no to?*

How to Use Opportunity Cost in Everyday Life

Next time you have a choice, stop and ask:

1. **What am I choosing?** (*What do I get?*)
2. **What am I giving up?** (*What's the cost?*)
3. **Which one is more valuable to me?** (*Is this the best use of my time, money, or energy?*)

Try It Yourself!

You're deciding whether to **play video games for an hour** or **practice a new skill** (like drawing or soccer).

- **Choice 1:** Play video games.
- **Choice 2:** Practice and get better at something.

If you choose video games, the **opportunity cost** is missing the chance to improve your skills. If you choose practice, the **opportunity cost** is not playing your game.

The Secret to Better Choices

Every decision has a cost—even if you don't see it right away. Smart decision-makers **think ahead** and choose what gives them the **best** result in the long run. Next time you make a choice, remember: **picking one thing means losing another — so, choose wisely!**

Chapter 11: The Eisenhower Matrix – What's Urgent vs. What's Important

Imagine you have **homework to finish, a birthday party to plan**, and **a new game you really want to play.** Everything feels like it needs to be done **right now**—but does it?

Some things feel urgent, but **not everything is equally important.** That's where the **Eisenhower Matrix** comes in—it helps you decide **what to do first, what can wait, and what isn't worth your time.**

Urgent vs. Important: What's the Difference?

- **Urgent** tasks need attention **right now**—like answering a ringing phone.
- **Important** tasks help you in the **long run**—like studying for a test or practicing a skill.

Some things are **both urgent and important** (like finishing a project before the deadline). But others **only feel urgent** (like checking every new text message).

How the Eisenhower Matrix Works

This tool helps you **sort your tasks** into four categories:

1. **Important & Urgent – Do It Now!**
    o   Homework due today
    o   Studying for a test tomorrow
    o   Helping someone in an emergency
2. **Important but Not Urgent – Plan It!**
    o   Practicing a sport or hobby
    o   Saving money for something big
    o   Building a good friendship
3. **Urgent but Not Important – Limit It!**
    o   Replying to random messages
    o   Watching a new video because everyone else is
    o   Doing small tasks that don't really matter
4. **Not Urgent & Not Important – Skip It!**
    o   Scrolling through your phone with no goal
    o   Playing a game just because you're bored
    o   Worrying about things you can't change

How to Use It in Real Life

Next time you feel **overwhelmed with things to do**, try this:

1. **Make a list of everything on your mind.**
2. **Sort each task** into one of the four categories.
3. **Start with the important and urgent tasks first.**
4. **Plan time for the important but not urgent tasks.**
5. **Cut down or remove the things that aren't worth your time.**

Try It Yourself!

You have a big test coming up, but your friend just texted asking if you want to play a game.

- **Important & Urgent:** Studying for your test.

- **Important but Not Urgent:** Practicing a hobby for fun.

- **Urgent but Not Important:** Replying to your friend's

text right away.

- **Not Urgent & Not Important:** Scrolling through memes instead of studying.

The Eisenhower Matrix helps you **focus on what really matters** so you don't waste time on things that don't.

The Secret to Getting More Done

Not everything that feels urgent is important. **Smart decision-makers focus on what truly matters.** When you manage your time wisely, you'll get more done *and* have time for fun—without stress!

Chapter 12: Regret Minimization – Avoiding "I Wish I Hadn't Done That" Moments

Have you ever made a decision and **immediately wished you could take it back**? Maybe you stayed up late watching YouTube videos and felt exhausted the next day. Or maybe you quit a game too early, only to find out your team made an amazing comeback.

Regret happens when we **make choices without thinking ahead**. But what if you could make decisions that **you won't regret later**? That's where **Regret Minimization** comes in! It helps you **think about the future before making a choice** so you don't end up saying, *"I wish I had done things differently."*

How to Use Regret Minimization

Before making a decision, ask yourself:

1. **How will I feel about this tomorrow?**
2. **How will I feel about this in a week?**
3. **How will I feel about this in a year?**

If you think your future self **will be happy** with your choice, go for it! If you think your future self **might regret it**, it's time to rethink.

Let's Try It!

Imagine you have a big school project due tomorrow, but your friend just invited you to go to the arcade.

- **Tomorrow:** You'll feel stressed trying to finish the project at the last minute.
- **A week from now:** You might regret your bad grade.
- **A year from now:** You probably won't even remember skipping the arcade, but you *will* remember struggling with your schoolwork.

Thinking ahead, you might **decide to finish the project first and plan another day to go to the arcade. That's how Regret Minimization helps you make smarter choices!**

Why This Works

Most regrets come from **acting too quickly** without considering what happens next. Regret Minimization **helps you slow down and think about the future** before making a decision.

The Secret to Fewer Regrets

Next time you're about to make a choice, **imagine your future self looking back.** If you think you'll **be proud of your decision**, go for it! If not, take a step back and make a different choice. **Your future self will thank you!**

Chapter 13: The Fermi Approach – Estimating When You Have No Clue

What if someone asked you, **"How many jellybeans fit in a giant jar?"** or **"How many people are playing soccer right now in your country?"**

You probably don't know the exact answer—but that doesn't mean you can't make a **smart guess!**

The **Fermi Approach** is a way of solving big or confusing problems by **breaking them into smaller, easier steps.** It helps you make good estimates —even when you have no clue where to start!

How the Fermi Approach Works

Instead of guessing randomly, the Fermi Approach asks:

1. **What do I already know?** (Even if it's not the exact answer, start with something related.)

2. **Can I break this into smaller parts?** (Big problems are easier to solve in steps.)

3. **Can I make a reasonable estimate?** (Think logically instead of randomly guessing.)

Imagine you want to estimate **how many slices of pizza are eaten in your city every day.**

- **Step 1: Start with what you know.** You know that many people like pizza and that most pizzas have about **8 slices.**
- **Step 2: Break it down.** How many people live in your city? Let's guess **500,000.** Maybe half of them eat pizza each day—so **250,000 people.**
- **Step 3: Make a smart estimate.** If each person eats **3 slices** on average, that's **250,000 × 3 = 750,000 slices of pizza every day!**

You might not get the exact number, but you're a lot **closer to the real answer** than a wild guess!

Why This Works

The Fermi Approach helps you:

- **Think logically instead of guessing randomly.**
- **Break big problems into smaller, solvable parts.**
- **Make good estimates even when you don't have all the facts.**

The Secret to Smarter Thinking

Next time you face a big question and don't know the answer, **don't panic!** Instead, use the Fermi Approach: **Start with what you know, break it down, and estimate step by step.** You'll be surprised how close you can get!

SECTION III
How to Avoid Thinking Traps

Your brain is amazing, but sometimes it **takes shortcuts that lead to mistakes.** These mistakes, called **thinking traps**, can trick you into making bad decisions without even realizing it! In this section, you'll learn about the **sneaky ways your brain can fool you** — and how to **outsmart these tricks** so you can make **better, smarter choices.** Let's start with one of the biggest thinking traps: **Anchoring Bias!**

Chapter 14: Anchoring Bias – The First Thing You Hear Isn't Always Right

Imagine you walk into a store and see a **cool backpack** with a price tag of **$100.** That sounds **expensive!** But then, you see another backpack that costs **$50.** Suddenly, the second one seems like a **great deal!**

But wait—**is it really a good deal, or does it just seem that way because of the first price you saw?**

This is called **Anchoring Bias.** It happens when your brain **gets stuck on the first piece of information you see**, even if it's not the most important.

How Anchoring Bias Tricks You

Your brain loves to **compare things** instead of judging them on their own. The first number, fact, or idea you see **sticks in your mind like an anchor**, making everything else seem better or worse in comparison.

Here's another example:

- A store lists a **video game at $60**, but then says, **"Now only $40!"** You feel like you're saving $20, but maybe the game was **never worth $60 to begin with!**
- A friend tells you a movie is **"the best ever,"** so you expect it to be amazing. But is it really, or did their opinion **anchor** your thinking?

Why It Matters

Anchoring Bias can lead to **bad decisions** because you're comparing things to **the first number or idea you saw, not what actually makes sense.** It can make you **spend more money, trust wrong information, or make choices too quickly.**

How to Avoid the Trap

1. **Slow down.** Just because something seems like a good deal doesn't mean it is. **Take a step back and think!**
2. **Compare wisely.** Instead of comparing something to the first number you see, **ask if it's truly worth it.**
3. **Look for more information.** Before deciding, **check other prices, opinions, or facts** so you don't get stuck on the first one.

Try It Yourself!

Let's say your friend tells you their favorite pizza place is **"the best in town."** Do you:

- **A:** Believe them without trying other places?
- **B:** Try different pizza places and decide for yourself?

The smart choice? **Option B!** That way, you're not just **anchored** to what they said—you're thinking for yourself!

The Secret to Avoiding Decision-making Traps

Anchoring Bias **tricks you into comparing instead of thinking.** Next time you see a "deal," hear an opinion, or get a big first number, **pause and ask: Is this really the best choice, or is my brain just stuck on the first thing I saw?**

Chapter 15: Confirmation Bias – Don't Just Believe What You Want to Be True

Have you ever been **sure** you were right about something—only to find out later you were wrong? Maybe you thought a test would be easy, so you only studied a little... and then realized too late that you **should have studied more.**

This happens because of **Confirmation Bias**—a sneaky thinking trap where your brain **only looks for information that proves what you already believe** and ignores everything else.

How Confirmation Bias Tricks You

Your brain **likes being right.** So instead of searching for the full truth, it tries to **find "proof" that your first thought was correct—even if it isn't!**

Here's an example:

- You think **your lucky socks** help you win soccer games. Every time you win while wearing them, you think, *See? They work!*

- But when you lose a game, you **ignore it** or make excuses: *That didn't count because it was raining.*
- Instead of seeing the whole picture (*winning depends on skill, practice, and teamwork*), your brain **only notices the times that "prove" you were right.**

Why This Is a Problem

Confirmation Bias can lead to **bad decisions** because it **blocks you from seeing the full truth.** It makes you:

- **Ignore facts that don't match what you already believe.**
- **Make decisions based on feelings instead of reality.**
- **Miss chances to learn and grow.**

How to Avoid This Trap

1. **Ask yourself, "Could I be wrong?"** Instead of looking for proof that you're right, look for **facts on both sides.**
2. **Check different sources.** If you hear something online, don't just believe the first thing you see—**look at different opinions and facts.**
3. **Listen to people who disagree with you.** Instead of arguing, **try to understand their point of view.** You might learn something new!

Try It Yourself!

Imagine you think **cats are better than dogs.** Instead of only watching videos about why cats are great, try looking up **why dogs are great too.** If you still like cats more, that's fine—but at least you **gave both sides a fair chance!**

The Secret to Smarter Thinking

Confirmation Bias **makes your brain look for "proof" that you're right—even when you're not.** To make better choices, **look at all the facts, not just the ones you like!** The more open you are to learning, the smarter your decisions will be.

Chapter 16: Availability Heuristic – Just Because It's Easy to Remember Doesn't Mean It's True

Imagine you're watching the news, and you see a story about a shark attack at the beach. Later, when your friends invite you to go swimming in the ocean, you say, **"No way! I don't want to get eaten by a shark!"**

But here's the thing—**shark attacks are extremely rare.** You're actually more likely to get hurt **by a falling coconut** than by a shark! So why does your brain make you think shark attacks are common?

This is called the **Availability Heuristic**—a thinking trap where your brain **believes something is more likely just because it's easier to remember.**

How the Availability Heuristic Tricks You

Your brain likes to **take shortcuts.** Instead of looking up facts, it **relies on the first thing that pops into your mind.**

Here are some ways this can trick you:

- **You see a plane crash on the news and think flying is dangerous. But actually, planes are much safer than cars!**
- **You remember one time you failed a test and think you're bad at math. But you've done well on plenty of tests—you just don't remember them as easily!**
- **You hear about one person getting sick from a certain food and decide never to eat it. But millions of people eat it safely every day.**

Why This Is a Problem

The Availability Heuristic makes you **trust your memory more than actual facts.** This can lead to:

- **Unnecessary fear** (*like thinking every stranger is dangerous just because of a scary news story*).
- **Bad decisions** (*like avoiding a great opportunity because of one bad experience*).
- **Wrong beliefs** (*like thinking something is true just because you heard it a lot*).

How to Avoid This Trap

1. **Ask, "Is this really common, or does it just feel that way?"** Just because you hear about something often **doesn't mean it happens a lot.**
2. **Look at the numbers.** If you're scared of something, **check the real facts** instead of going with what you remember.
3. **Think about the good, not just the bad.** Your brain remembers negative things more easily, so **make sure you're looking at the full picture.**

Try It Yourself!

Let's say your friend thinks roller coasters are unsafe because they heard about **one accident.** Instead of agreeing right away, you check the facts and find out that **millions of people ride roller coasters safely every year.** Now you can **decide based on facts, not just fear.**

The Secret to Avoiding This Trap

The Availability Heuristic **makes you believe things are more common just because they're easier to remember.** Next time your brain jumps to a conclusion, **pause and check the facts.** The real answer might surprise you!

Chapter 17: Sunk Cost Fallacy – Why Holding Onto Mistakes Makes Them Worse

Imagine you're playing a board game, but **halfway through, you realize you don't like it.** You'd rather do something else, but you think, *I've already spent an hour playing... I might as well finish.*

Or maybe you start reading a book, but it's **boring.** Instead of putting it down, you tell yourself, *I've already read half of it—I can't stop now!*

This is called the **Sunk Cost Fallacy.** It's a thinking trap where **you keep doing something just because you've already spent time, money, or effort on it—even if it's not the best choice anymore.**

How the Sunk Cost Fallacy Tricks You

Your brain doesn't like to **waste things.** If you've **put in time or effort**, you feel like quitting means **you've lost everything.**

Here's how this thinking trap works:

- **You spend money on a movie ticket, but the movie is terrible.** Instead of leaving, you think, *I paid for this, so I have to stay.*
- **You keep playing a video game you don't enjoy anymore** because you've already played for hours.
- **You eat food you don't like** just because you already paid for it.

Why This Is a Problem

The Sunk Cost Fallacy **makes you stick with bad decisions** just because you've already spent something on them. But here's the truth:

- **Time you've already spent is gone—you can't get it back.**
- **Money you've already used is spent—you can't unspend it.**
- **Forcing yourself to finish something you don't enjoy just wastes more time!**

How to Avoid This Trap

1. **Ask, "Would I start this now?"** If you weren't already doing it, **would you choose to do it?** If not, it's okay to stop.

2. **Focus on the future, not the past.** Instead of thinking, *What have I already spent?* ask, *What's the best choice moving forward?*

3. **Let go of bad choices.** Just because you **started something** doesn't mean you have to **finish** if it's not worth it anymore.

Let's say you've been **watching a TV show, but you don't like it anymore.**

- **Stuck in the trap:** *I've already watched three seasons, so I have to finish!*
- **Smart choice:** *That time is already spent—I can stop and do something better with my time.*

How to Avoid Getting Stuck

The Sunk Cost Fallacy **makes you afraid to quit, even when quitting is the smarter choice.** Next time you feel stuck, **forget what you've already spent and focus on what's best for your future.** Sometimes, the smartest decision is to **walk away!**

Chapter 18: Overconfidence Bias – Thinking You Know More Than You Do

Have you ever been **super sure** about something — only to find out later that you were **completely wrong**? Maybe you thought you knew all the answers to a test but got a lower grade than expected. Or maybe you were sure you could beat your friend in a video game without practicing, only to lose big time.

This happens because of **Overconfidence Bias** — a thinking trap where **you believe you know more than you actually do.**

How Overconfidence Bias Tricks You

Your brain **likes to feel smart** and **in control.** But sometimes, it **tricks you into thinking you know everything—** even when you don't!

Here are some common examples:

- **You don't study for a test** because you assume you already know everything—then you struggle with the harder questions.

- **You jump into a new game without reading the rules** and quickly realize you don't know how to play.
- **You guess an answer instead of double-checking it—** and get it wrong.

Being confident is **good**, but **being overconfident** can lead to mistakes.

Why This Is a Problem

Overconfidence Bias makes you:

- **Take shortcuts** instead of preparing properly.
- **Ignore advice** from people who might actually know more.
- **Underestimate challenges**, making things harder for yourself.

How to Avoid This Trap

1. **Ask, "Do I really know this, or am I just guessing?"** If you're not 100% sure, take a moment to check.
2. **Listen to feedback.** If someone corrects you, don't ignore them—see if they might be right.
3. **Be open to learning.** Even if you think you know a lot, there's always more to discover.

Try It Yourself!

Imagine you're about to race your friend in a new game. You think, *I don't need to learn the rules—I'll figure it out!*

- **Stuck in the trap:** You lose because you didn't take the time to learn the game first.
- **Smart choice:** You ask about the rules and **practice first**—giving you a much better chance to win.

How To Stay Curious

Overconfidence Bias **makes you think you know more than you actually do.** The best way to avoid it? **Stay curious, double-check your facts, and always be open to learning!** Smart people don't just assume they're right—they take the time to **make sure.**

Chapter 19: The Framing Effect – How Words Can Trick You

Imagine you're at the grocery store, and you see two signs on cartons of juice:

- **Option 1:** "90% real fruit juice!"
- **Option 2:** "Only 10% sugar water!"

Which one would you pick?

Most people choose **Option 1** because "90% real fruit juice" *sounds* better. But guess what?

Both are the exact same thing! The way something is **described** can **change how your brain sees it—even when the facts don't change.**

This is called the **Framing Effect**, and it's a sneaky trick that **makes you feel differently about something just because of how it's worded.**

How the Framing Effect Tricks You

Your brain reacts differently depending on **how something is said**, not just what it means. Let's look at another example:

- **A doctor says, "This medicine helps 80 out of 100 people feel better."** You feel hopeful.
- **A doctor says, "This medicine doesn't work for 20 out of 100 people."** You feel unsure.

Both statements mean the **same thing**, but one *sounds* much better than the other. That's the **Framing Effect** at work!

Why This Is a Problem

The Framing Effect can make you:

- **Believe something is better or worse than it really is.**
- **Trust a deal or discount that sounds amazing—even if it's not that special.**
- **Get scared by how something is worded, even if the facts aren't so bad.**

How to Avoid This Trap

1. **Flip the wording.** If something sounds too good (or too bad) to be true, **try saying it the opposite way** and see if it still makes sense.
2. **Look at the actual facts.** Instead of reacting to how something is **described**, check what's actually true.
3. **Ask, "Is this trying to change how I feel?"** If something is **framed to sound exciting or scary**, stop and think before believing it.

Try It Yourself!

Imagine you're buying a snack, and the label says:

- **Option 1:** "80% fat-free!"
- **Option 2:** "Contains 20% fat."

Which one sounds healthier? The first one *sounds* better, but **both are exactly the same!** That's the Framing Effect in action.

The Framing Effect **changes how things sound without changing the truth.** Next time you hear something that seems *too good or too scary*, **pause and look at the facts.** When you see through the trick, you make **smarter, clearer choices!**

Chapter 20: Loss Aversion – Why Losing Feels Worse Than Winning Feels Good

Have you ever found a dollar on the ground? That feels pretty awesome! But now imagine you had a dollar in your pocket, and you **lost** it. That would feel **way worse** than finding a dollar felt good.

That's because of **Loss Aversion**—a sneaky brain trick that makes **losing something feel much worse than gaining the same thing.**

How Loss Aversion Tricks You

Your brain **hates losing** so much that it sometimes **makes bad choices just to avoid it.**

Here are some examples:

- **You keep playing a board game you don't like** just because you already spent an hour on it. (*I don't want to waste my time!*)

- **You hold onto toys you don't play with** because giving them away *feels like losing something—even if you never use them!*

- **You wait in a long line for a ride** even though another ride has no wait—because you don't want to "lose" the time you've already spent waiting.

Why This Can Be a Problem

Loss Aversion **makes you focus too much on what you might lose instead of what you could gain.** It can cause you to:

- **Stay stuck doing things you don't enjoy.**
- **Make choices based on fear instead of what's actually best.**
- **Say "yes" to things just because you don't want to miss out.**

How to Stop This Thinking Trap

1. **Ask, "Would I make this choice if I were starting fresh?"** If the only reason you're sticking with something is because you don't want to "lose," that's a sign to rethink your choice.

2. **Think about what you'll gain instead.** If you stop playing a boring game, now you have time for a fun one! If you give away an old toy, someone else can enjoy it, and you have more space for things you actually use.

3. **Remember: Losing isn't always bad.** Sometimes letting go of one thing makes space for **something even better.**

Try It Yourself!

Imagine you're **reading a book that's boring.**

- **Loss Aversion says:** *I already read 50 pages, so I have to finish it.*

- **Smart thinking says:** *That time is already gone—why not spend the rest of my time reading something fun instead?*

How to Make Better Choices

Loss Aversion makes losing **feel worse than it really is.** But sometimes, **letting go of one thing helps you get something even better!** Next time you don't want to give something up, **ask yourself if it's really worth keeping — or if it's time to move on.**

Chapter 21: Hindsight Bias – Thinking You "Knew It All Along"

Have you ever watched a game and, after your team lost, thought, **"I knew they were going to lose!"** Or maybe you guessed an answer on a test and got it wrong, then told yourself, **"I knew I should have picked the other one!"**

That's called **Hindsight Bias**—a sneaky brain trick that makes you **think you knew something was going to happen... even though you actually didn't.**

How Hindsight Bias Tricks You

Your brain loves to feel **smart and in control.** So when something happens, it **rewrites the past** to make it seem like you "knew it all along"—even if you didn't!

Here's how this thinking trap works:

- **Before a race:** You aren't sure who will win.
- **After the race:** You say, *"I knew that runner would win!"* (Even though you really didn't!)

Or:

- **Before a test:** You aren't sure of an answer.
- **After the test:** You think, *"I knew I should have picked the other answer!"* (But if you really *knew*, you would have picked it the first time!)

Why This Can Be a Problem

Hindsight Bias **makes you feel like you were right all along**, which can **stop you from learning from mistakes.** If you always think, *"I knew that was going to happen,"* you might:

- Ignore what you actually learned.
- Forget that some things are just unpredictable.
- Miss a chance to improve your decision-making.

How to Avoid This Trap

1. **Be honest about what you really knew.** If you didn't predict something, admit it—don't trick yourself into thinking you did!

2. **Remember that some things are impossible to know.** No one can predict the future 100% of the time.

3. **Learn from what happened.** Instead of saying, *"I knew it,"* ask, *"What can I learn for next time?"*

Try It Yourself!

Imagine you flip a coin. Before flipping, you guess **heads**. It lands on **tails.**

- **Hindsight Bias says:** *"I knew it was going to be tails!"* (But you didn't—you just wish you had guessed differently.)
- **Smart thinking says:** *"I couldn't have known—it was a 50/50 chance."*

How to Think Smarter

Hindsight Bias **makes you believe you "knew" something after it already happened.** But real learning happens when you admit what you **didn't know** and use that knowledge to make **better choices next time.** Instead of saying, *"I knew it all along,"* start asking, *"What can I learn from this?"*

Chapter 22: Groupthink – When Everyone Just Follows the Crowd

Have you ever been in a group where everyone **agrees on something**, even if it doesn't seem like the best idea? Maybe your friends all decide to play a game you don't like, but you go along with it because **you don't want to be the only one who disagrees.**

That's called **Groupthink**—a thinking trap where people **just follow the group instead of thinking for themselves.**

How Groupthink Tricks You

Your brain **wants to fit in.** It doesn't like feeling **left out** or being the only one with a different opinion. So instead of saying, *"I don't think this is a good idea,"* your brain says, *"Just go along with it so no one gets upset."*

Here's how this trap works:

- **Everyone in your class likes a new movie, but you don't.** You pretend to like it so you don't feel different.

- **Your friends want to skip practice, even though you know you should go.** You don't say anything because you don't want to be the only one who disagrees.

- **A group is making a bad choice, but no one speaks up.** Everyone assumes, *"If no one else is saying anything, it must be fine."*

Why This Can Be a Problem

Groupthink can lead to **bad decisions** because no one stops to ask, *"Is this really a good idea?"* It can make you:

- **Do things you wouldn't normally do.**
- **Ignore your own opinions because you're afraid to be different.**
- **Miss out on making better choices.**

How to Avoid This Trap

1. **Ask yourself, "Do I really agree, or am I just going along with the group?"**
2. **Speak up if something doesn't feel right.** Others might be thinking the same thing but are also afraid to say it!
3. **Remember, it's okay to have a different opinion.** Being part of a group **doesn't** mean you have to agree with everything.

Try It Yourself!

Imagine your friends want to sneak snacks into the movies, but you know it's against the rules.

- **Groupthink says:** *"Everyone else is doing it, so I should too."*
- **Smart thinking says:** *"Just because they're doing it doesn't mean I have to."*

The Power of Thinking for Yourself

Groupthink **makes people follow the crowd without thinking.** But **great decision-makers aren't afraid to think for themselves!** Next time you feel pressured to go along with something, **pause and ask yourself if it's really the best choice.** Sometimes, the smartest person in the room is the one who speaks up!

Chapter 23: The Dunning-Kruger Effect – Thinking You're a Genius (When You're Not)

Have you ever met someone who **thinks they're an expert at something—but really isn't?** Maybe a friend brags about being great at a video game, but when they play, they lose **every round.** Or maybe someone claims they "know everything" about a subject but gets a lot of facts wrong.

That's called the **Dunning-Kruger Effect**—a thinking trap where **people who don't know much about something believe they know a lot.**

How the Dunning-Kruger Effect Tricks You

When people learn **a little** about a topic, they sometimes feel **overconfident**—because they don't know enough to realize how much they're actually missing!

Here's how this works:

1. **You try something new and do okay at first.** (*This is easy! I must be great at this!*)

2. **You feel super confident, even though you don't know much yet.** (*I already know enough—I don't need to learn more!*)

3. **Later, you realize it's harder than you thought.** (*Oh... maybe I didn't know as much as I thought!*)

Why This Can Be a Problem

The Dunning-Kruger Effect **tricks you into thinking you're better at something than you really are.** This can lead to:

- **Skipping practice because you think you don't need it.**
- **Not listening to advice from people who actually know more.**
- **Making mistakes because you didn't take time to learn properly.**

How to Avoid This Trap

1. **Ask yourself, "Do I really know enough, or should I learn more?"** If you've only just started something, there's probably **a lot more to learn!**

2. **Listen to experts.** If someone with more experience gives advice, **pay attention instead of assuming you already know best.**

3. **Keep practicing.** The best way to improve is to **keep learning, even if you think you're already good.**

Try It Yourself!

Imagine you've played a game **a few times** and think you're amazing at it. But then you play against an expert and **lose quickly.**

- **Dunning-Kruger Effect says:** *"That was just bad luck. I'm still really good."*
- **Smart thinking says:** *"Maybe I have more to learn! I should watch how they play and improve."*

The Best Way to Get Smarter

The Dunning-Kruger Effect **makes people think they know more than they do.** But truly smart people **always keep learning!** The next time you feel like an expert at something, **ask yourself if there's more to discover.** The more you learn, the better you'll really be!

SECTION IV
Decision-Making Tools for Kids

Making smart choices isn't just about avoiding thinking traps—it's also about using the **right tools to help you decide.** Just like a builder needs a hammer and a scientist needs a microscope, **great decision-makers use special thinking tools** to make the best choices. In this section, you'll learn **simple and powerful tricks** that can help you **solve problems, compare options, and make better decisions—every time!** Let's start with the **Decision Tree,** a tool that helps you see **where your choices might lead!**

Chapter 24: The Decision Tree – How to Plan Your Choices Step-by-Step

Imagine you're in a maze. At every turn, you have two paths to choose from. Some paths lead to **treasure**, and others lead to **dead ends**. If you could see the whole maze **before you started**, wouldn't it be easier to find the best way through?

That's exactly what a **Decision Tree** does! It helps you **see your choices, think about what might happen, and pick the smartest path.**

How a Decision Tree Works

A Decision Tree is like a map for your choices. Instead of guessing, you write down your options and what could happen next.

Here's how to make one:

1. **Start with your decision.** What are you trying to choose? (*Example: Should I spend my money or save it?*)

2. **Write your options.** List the choices you have. (*Spend it now or save it?*)

3. **Think ahead.** For each choice, write what could happen next. (*If I spend it, I get something now but might regret it later. If I save it, I can buy something even better later!*)

4. **Pick the best path.** Look at your options and choose the one that leads to the best result!

Let's Try It!

Imagine you're deciding whether to **do your homework now or later.**

- **Choice 1: Do it now. → You nish early → You have free time later with no stress!**
- **Choice 2: Do it later. → You feel rushed before bedtime → You're tired and don't do your best work.**

Looking at the Decision Tree, **doing homework now is clearly the better choice!**

Why This Works

Using a Decision Tree helps you:

- **See the future before making a choice.**
- **Avoid bad decisions that lead to problems.**
- **Pick the smartest path instead of guessing.**

A Smart Way to Make Decisions

Next time you have a tricky choice, **draw a Decision Tree!** When you see where each path leads, it's much easier to **make the best decision — and avoid dead ends!**

Chapter 25: The Six Thinking Hats – Seeing a Problem in Different Ways

Imagine you're trying to solve a problem, but everyone in the room has **a different opinion.** One person is **excited**, another is **worried**, someone else is **super logical**, and another just **wants to be creative.** How do you **figure out the best decision** when everyone thinks differently?

That's where the **Six Thinking Hats** method comes in! It's a fun and simple way to **look at a decision from different angles** so you can see the **full picture** before choosing.

What Are the Six Thinking Hats?

Each **Thinking Hat** represents a different way of thinking. When making a decision, you can **"wear" each hat one at a time** to consider all sides.

- **Yellow Hat (Positives)** – What's good about this idea? What are the benefits?
- **Black Hat (Negatives)** – What could go wrong? Are there any risks?

- **Blue Hat (Planning)** – What steps do we need to take to make this work?
- **Red Hat (Feelings)** – How do I feel about this? What does my gut say?
- **Green Hat (Creativity)** – Can I think of a new or different way to do this?
- **White Hat (Facts & Information)** – What do I know? What are the facts?

Let's Try It!

Imagine you're trying to decide whether to **start a lemonade stand.** Let's "wear" each hat and see what it tells us!

- **Yellow Hat:** I could make money and learn how to run a business!
- **Black Hat:** What if no one buys my lemonade? I could lose money.
- **Blue Hat:** I'll need lemons, cups, a table, and a sign to get started.
- **Red Hat:** I feel excited, but a little nervous too!
- **Green Hat:** Maybe I could sell cookies too to attract more customers!
- **White Hat:** It's summer, and people like cold drinks—so it's a good time to try!

By using **all six hats**, you get a **clearer picture** of what might happen instead of only looking at it one way.

Why This Works

The Six Thinking Hats help you:

- **Consider different perspectives before deciding.**
- **Spot problems before they happen.**
- **Find creative solutions instead of only seeing obstacles.**

A Fun Way to Make Better Decisions

Next time you're making a big choice, **try using the Six Thinking Hats!** Looking at a decision from every angle helps you **see things clearly—and make the smartest choice!**

Chapter 26: SWOT Analysis – Strengths, Weaknesses, Opportunities, and Threats

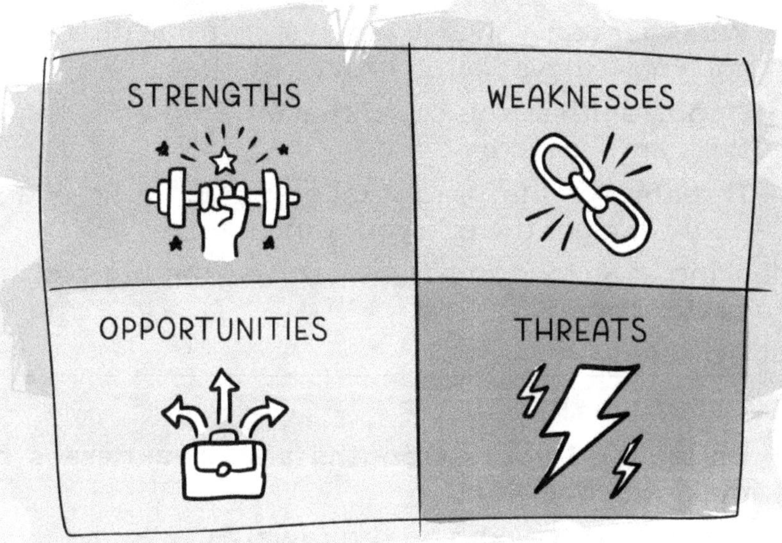

Imagine you're deciding whether to **try out for the school play.** You love acting, but you're also a little nervous. How do you figure out if it's the right choice?

A **SWOT Analysis** is a tool that helps you **weigh the good and bad** before making a decision. It stands for:

- **Strengths** – What are you good at? What will help you succeed?
- **Weaknesses** – What might be hard for you? What could hold you back?
- **Opportunities** – What good things could come from this choice?
- **Threats** – What challenges or risks should you watch out for?

How to Use a SWOT Analysis

A SWOT Analysis helps you **think through a decision step by step** instead of just guessing.

Let's try it with the school play example.

- **Strengths:** You love performing, you're creative, and you remember lines easily.
- **Weaknesses:** You get nervous in front of big crowds, and you've never acted on stage before.
- **Opportunities:** You could make new friends, learn new skills, and gain confidence.
- **Threats:** The play might take up a lot of time, and you might not get the role you want.

By looking at all four areas, you can **see the big picture** and make a **better choice.**

Why This Works

A SWOT Analysis helps you:

- **Understand your strengths and weaknesses before making a decision.**
- **See both the risks and the rewards.**
- **Make a choice based on facts instead of just feelings.**

Try It Yourself!

Imagine you're deciding whether to **join the soccer team.** Before saying yes or no, write down your:

- **Strengths** – Are you fast? Do you enjoy teamwork?
- **Weaknesses** – Do you get tired quickly? Are you new to the sport?
- **Opportunities** – Will you learn new skills? Make new friends?
- **Threats** – Will it take too much time? Could you get injured?

A Simple Way to Make Smarter Choices

The next time you have a big decision, **use a SWOT Analysis!** It helps you see **both the good and the bad** so you can choose wisely and feel **confident** in your decision!

Chapter 27: Pro/Con Lists Done Right – Why Writing It Down Helps

Factor	Pro/Con	Weight	Impact	Score
Go to sleepover	Pro	9	+8	+72
Be popular with friends	Pro	8	+7	+56
Might not sleep well	Con	7	-6	-42
Far from family	Con	6	-5	-30
Pros Total: +128	Cons Total: -72		Net Score: +56	

Have you ever had **two choices** and felt stuck on which one to pick? Maybe you're trying to decide whether to **go to a sleepover or stay home for a family movie night.** Both sound fun, so how do you choose?

A **Pro/Con List** is a simple way to **see the good and bad of each option** by writing them down. When you see your choices clearly, making a decision becomes **much easier!**

How to Make a Pro/Con List

A **Pro** is something **good** about a choice.

A **Con** is something **not so good** about it.

Let's say you're deciding whether to go to the sleepover or stay home.

Option 1: Go to the Sleepover

Pros:

- You get to hang out with friends.
- You'll have fun playing games and watching movies.
- You might make great memories.

Cons:

- You might not sleep well.
- You could miss your family's movie night.
- You have an early soccer game the next morning.

Option 2: Stay Home for Family Movie Night

Pros:

- You'll be well-rested for soccer.
- You get to spend time with family.
- You don't have to pack an overnight bag.

Cons:

- You'll miss the fun with friends.
- You might feel left out if they talk about it later.

Why This Works

A Pro/Con List helps you:

- **See your choices clearly instead of just guessing.**
- **Think about what really matters most.**
- **Make a smart decision you'll be happy with later.**

Try It Yourself!

The next time you're stuck between two choices, grab a piece of paper and **write down the pros and cons.** You might be surprised at how **much easier** your decision becomes!

A Simple Trick for Smarter Decisions

Sometimes, a choice feels difficult just because you haven't **seen it on paper.** Writing down the pros and cons helps you **stop overthinking and start deciding.** Try it next time, and see how much clearer your choices become!

Chapter 28: Scenario Planning – Imagining What Could Go Right (or Wrong)

Have you ever made a choice and later thought, **"I didn't expect that to happen!"**? Maybe you went outside without a jacket because it looked sunny, but then it started raining. Or maybe you picked a hard level in a game without checking what you needed, and you lost right away.

That's where **Scenario Planning** helps! It's a decision-making tool that lets you **think ahead and imagine different outcomes** before making a choice.

How Scenario Planning Works

Instead of just picking something and hoping for the best, **Scenario Planning helps you ask, "What could happen next?"**

Here's how to do it:

1. **Think about your decision.** What are you trying to choose? (*Example: Should I bring an umbrella today?*)

2. **Imagine different scenarios.** What are the possible outcomes? (*It might stay sunny, or it could rain.*)
3. **Decide what's smartest based on the possibilities.** (*Since rain is possible, it's better to bring an umbrella just in case!*)

Let's Try It!

Imagine you're deciding whether to **ride your bike to school or take the bus.**

- **Scenario 1:** You ride your bike, and the weather stays nice. *Great choice!*
- **Scenario 2:** You ride your bike, but it starts raining. *Now you're wet and uncomfortable!*
- **Scenario 3:** You take the bus, and it turns out to be a super hot day. *You avoided sweating on your bike ride!*

After thinking through the scenarios, you **might decide to check the weather before choosing.**

Why This Works

Scenario Planning helps you:

- **Avoid surprises by thinking ahead.**
- **Make smarter choices based on different possibilities.**
- **Be prepared for whatever happens!**

Try It Yourself!

The next time you have a decision to make, ask yourself:

- *What are the different things that could happen?*
- *Will I still be happy with my choice in each situation?*
- *How can I prepare for the best and worst outcomes?*

A Clever Way to Avoid Surprises

Scenario Planning **helps you think ahead instead of guessing.** The more you practice imagining different outcomes, the better you'll be at making choices that **work out well — no matter what happens!**

Chapter 29: Pre-Mortem Analysis – Thinking About Failing Before It Happens

Have you ever started something **only to realize later that you made a big mistake**? Maybe you forgot to bring supplies for a school project, or you started a game without checking the rules and lost quickly.

Wouldn't it be great if you could **spot mistakes before they happen?** That's exactly what **Pre-Mortem Analysis** helps you do! It's a simple way to **imagine what could go wrong before you make a decision** so you can fix problems before they happen.

How Pre-Mortem Analysis Works

Instead of only thinking, *What if this goes well?*, you also ask, *What if this goes wrong?* Then, you figure out how to **avoid those problems before they happen.**

Here's how to do it:

1. **Imagine you made your decision—and it completely failed.** What went wrong?
2. **List all the possible reasons for the failure.** Did you forget something? Did you not prepare enough?
3. **Make a plan to prevent those mistakes.** Now that you know what could go wrong, you can fix it before it happens!

Let's Try It!

Imagine you are about to **give a class presentation.** Instead of just hoping it goes well, you do a Pre-Mortem Analysis.

- **Possible failure:** You forget what to say in the middle of the presentation.
- **Solution:** Practice in front of a mirror or with a friend so you feel more confident.
- **Possible failure:** The slideshow doesn't work.
- **Solution:** Print out notes so you can continue even if the screen doesn't load.

By thinking ahead, you **catch problems before they happen** and have a plan to handle them!

Why This Works

Pre-Mortem Analysis helps you:

- **Prepare for problems instead of being surprised by them.**
- **Feel more confident because you're ready for anything.**
- **Make smarter choices by avoiding mistakes before they happen.**

A Smart Way to Stay One Step Ahead

The next time you make a big decision, **imagine what could go wrong first.** When you plan for problems before they happen, you'll always be **one step ahead—and ready to succeed!**

Chapter 30: Heuristic Shortcuts – Quick Thinking, but Smarter

Have you ever **made a quick decision without really thinking about it?** Maybe you always pick the same snack at lunch because you know you like it. Or maybe you guessed the answer on a test because it "felt right."

Your brain **likes to save time**, so it uses **shortcuts** to help you make choices quickly. These shortcuts are called **heuristics**—they help you **think fast**, but sometimes they can **lead you in the wrong direction.**

How Heuristic Shortcuts Work

Your brain takes **shortcuts** so you don't have to stop and think about every little thing.

Here are some common shortcuts:

- **The Familiarity Shortcut** – You pick something just because you know it. (*Example: You always choose pepperoni pizza because it's what you usually eat—even though another flavor might be great!*)

- **The Popularity Shortcut** – You assume something is good just because lots of people like it. (*Example: Everyone at school is wearing a certain brand of shoes, so you think you need them too.*)
- **The First Answer Shortcut** – You believe the first thing you hear. (*Example: Your friend tells you a new kid is mean, so you believe it without getting to know them yourself.*)

When Heuristics Help

Sometimes, heuristics make life **easier and faster.**

- **Choosing clothes in the morning** – You don't need to try on everything in your closet.
- **Finding your favorite cereal at the store** – You grab it without reading every box.
- **Staying safe** – If something looks dangerous, you move away fast instead of stopping to think.

When Heuristics Cause Mistakes

But **fast thinking isn't always smart thinking.**

- **You assume a game will be fun** just because the cover looks cool.
- **You think you know the answer on a test** without reading the question carefully.
- **You believe a rumor** because you heard it from one person instead of checking if it's true.

How to Use Heuristics Wisely

1. **Pause before making a fast decision.** Ask yourself, *Am I choosing this just because it's easy?*
2. **Check the facts.** If something sounds unbelievable, make sure it's true before you believe it.
3. **Trust shortcuts only when they make sense.** If a decision is important, **slow down and think it through.**

Imagine your friend tells you a **new movie is boring** before you even see it.

- **Fast thinking says:** "I won't watch it—it must be bad!"
- **Smart thinking says:** "Maybe I should see it for myself before deciding!"

How to Think Fast Without Making Mistakes

Heuristics help you **make quick choices**, but they can also **lead you the wrong way.** The key is to **know when to trust them—and when to slow down and think.** Smart decision-makers **use shortcuts wisely** instead of letting shortcuts **control their thinking!**

SECTION V
Emotions and Decision-Making

Making choices isn't just about **thinking logically**—your **feelings** play a big role too! Sometimes, emotions **help you make good decisions**, like feeling excited about trying something new. But other times, emotions can **push you into bad choices**, like saying something mean when you're angry. In this section, you'll learn how to **balance your feelings with smart thinking** so you can make decisions that you won't regret later!

Chapter 31: Self-Regulation – Keeping Your Feelings in Check

Have you ever **said or done something you regretted** just because you were mad, sad, or frustrated? Maybe you **shouted at a friend** when you were upset or **quit a game** because you lost. Later, you probably thought, *I wish I had handled that better!*

That's where **self-regulation** comes in. It means **controlling your emotions instead of letting them control you.** It helps you **stay calm, think clearly, and make better choices — even when you're feeling strong emotions.**

How Emotions Can Lead to Bad Choices

When emotions take over, **it's easy to make mistakes.**

- **Anger:** You snap at a friend without thinking, then feel bad later.
- **Fear:** You don't try something new because you're scared you'll fail.
- **Excitement:** You rush into a decision without thinking about the consequences.

How to Stay in Control

Instead of letting emotions **push you into bad choices**, use these simple tricks to stay in control:

1. **Pause before reacting.** If you feel a strong emotion, **take a deep breath** and give yourself a few seconds to think.

2. **Name your feeling.** Say to yourself, *I'm feeling angry* or *I'm feeling nervous.* Just recognizing your emotion can help you handle it better.

3. **Ask yourself, "What happens next?"** Think about what will happen if you act on your emotion. Will you regret it?

4. **Find a way to calm down.** If you're too upset to think clearly, try taking a walk, listening to music, or counting to ten.

Try It Yourself!

Imagine your little brother **takes your favorite toy without asking.**

- **Reacting without control:** You yell and grab it back, making him cry.

- **Using self-regulation:** You take a deep breath and calmly tell him, *Please ask next time.*

Why This Matters

Self-regulation **helps you make better decisions, avoid regrets, and handle tough situations with confidence.** The more you practice it, the easier it gets! Instead of letting your emotions **take over**, you'll learn to **stay in control and choose wisely.**

Chapter 32: Empathy and Decisions – Thinking About Others Before You Choose

Have you ever made a decision that seemed good for you—but later realized it **hurt someone else**? Maybe you **grabbed the last piece of cake** without asking if anyone else wanted it, or you **chose a game that you liked** but your friend didn't enjoy.

That's where **empathy** comes in. Empathy means **understanding how someone else feels.** It helps you make decisions that aren't just good for you—but also **kind and fair to others.**

How Empathy Helps You Make Better Choices

Before making a decision, empathy helps you **stop and think about how it affects others.**

Let's say you're deciding whether to:

- **Take the biggest cookie for yourself.** (*How will that make others feel?*)

- **Interrupt a friend while they're talking.** (*Would I like it if someone did that to me?*)
- **Leave someone out of a game.** (*How would I feel if I were them?*)

By thinking about how your actions **affect others**, you can **make better choices that keep everyone happy.**

How to Use Empathy in Your Decisions

Before making a choice, ask yourself:

1. **How would I feel if this happened to me?**
2. **Will my choice hurt someone else's feelings?**
3. **Is there a way to make a fairer decision?**

Try It Yourself!

Imagine your friend really wants to play a board game, but you want to play video games instead.

- **Without empathy:** You ignore their idea and play what you want.
- **With empathy:** You take turns so both of you get to play what you enjoy.

Why This Matters

Empathy **helps you be a better friend, teammate, and family member.** It makes sure that your choices **aren't just good for you, but also fair and kind to others.** When you use empathy in decision-making, **everyone wins!**

Chapter 33: The Role of Intuition – When Your Gut Feeling Is (or Isn't) Right

Have you ever had a feeling deep inside that told you what to do—even when you weren't sure why? Maybe you met someone new and instantly felt like you could trust them, or you got a weird feeling about a situation and decided to walk away.

That feeling is called **intuition**, or your **gut feeling**. It's like a little voice in your head that **helps you make quick decisions** without thinking too hard. But here's the trick—sometimes your gut is **right**, and sometimes it **leads you the wrong way!**

When You Should Trust Your Gut

Intuition works best when your brain **recognizes patterns** from past experiences.

You can trust your gut when:

- **You've practiced something a lot.** If you've played soccer for years, your gut will often help you make quick moves without thinking.
- **You sense danger.** If a situation **feels wrong**, your brain might be picking up on something you don't fully understand.
- **You're making a simple decision.** If you're picking between two ice cream flavors, your gut can quickly tell you which one you like more!

When Your Gut Might Be Wrong

Intuition isn't always right, especially when:

- **You're in a new situation.** Your gut can't guide you well if you've never been in this situation before.
- **Emotions are controlling your decision.** If you're **angry, scared, or too excited**, your gut might push you to make a bad choice.
- **You're making a big, important decision.** Choosing a school, spending money, or making a big commitment **needs more than just a gut feeling—you need to think it through!**

How to Use Intuition the Smart Way

Before trusting your gut, ask yourself:

1. **Have I been in this situation before?** (*If yes, my gut might be right! If no, I should think more before deciding.*)
2. **Am I feeling emotional right now?** (*If I'm upset, I should slow down and think instead of rushing my decision.*)
3. **Is this a big decision?** (*For big choices, I should gather facts and not just rely on my feelings.*)

Try It Yourself!

Imagine your friends want to explore a shortcut through the woods, but something **feels off** about it.

- **Listening to your gut:** You decide not to go because your gut tells you it might not be safe. Later, you find out it was full of poison ivy!

- **Not listening to your gut:** You ignore the weird feeling and go anyway, ending up itchy for days.

The Right Way to Trust Your Gut

Intuition **can be a powerful tool, but it's not always right.** The best decision-makers know when to **listen to their gut —** **and when to slow down and think things through.** The next time you have a gut feeling, **pause and check if it's leading you in the right direction!**

Chapter 34: Dealing with Decision Fatigue – Why Too Many Choices Make You Tired

Have you ever felt so **tired of making decisions** that you just **pick anything to get it over with**? Maybe you spent all day choosing what to wear, what to eat, what game to play, and then by the end of the day, when someone asks, *"What do you want for dinner?"* you just say, **"I don't care!"**

That's called **Decision Fatigue**—when your brain gets **tired from making too many choices**, and you start making **lazy or bad decisions** just because you don't want to think anymore.

Why Too Many Choices Make You Tired

Your brain **uses energy every time you make a decision**—even for small things like picking a snack or choosing a song. The more choices you make in a day, the **more tired your brain gets.**

Here's what happens when Decision Fatigue kicks in:

- **You make random choices** just to get it over with. (*Example: You grab the first snack you see instead of picking something healthy.*)
- **You avoid making a choice at all.** (*Example: You can't decide what to watch, so you just sit there doing nothing.*)
- **You go for the easiest option—even if it's not the best.** (*Example: You pick a book for a school project that you don't even like, just because you don't want to think anymore.*)

How to Beat Decision Fatigue

Instead of letting your brain get **tired and overwhelmed**, use these tricks to make choices **easier**:

1. **Make fewer decisions.** If you don't have to choose, don't! (*Example: Wear the same favorite outfit each Monday so you don't have to think about it!*)
2. **Decide important things early.** If you wait until you're tired, you'll make worse choices. (*Example: Pack your lunch the night before instead of deciding in the morning when you're sleepy.*)
3. **Use routines.** If you do something the same way every time, your brain doesn't have to think about it. (*Example: Always do homework right after school so you don't have to decide when to start.*)

Try It Yourself!

Imagine you're picking a movie to watch.

- **With Decision Fatigue:** You scroll for 30 minutes, feel exhausted, and pick something random you don't even like.
- **Without Decision Fatigue:** You make a list of your favorite movies **beforehand**, so next time, you just choose from your list in seconds!

The more choices you make in a day, **the harder it gets to make good ones.** The trick to avoiding Decision Fatigue is to **simplify your choices, plan ahead, and use routines** so your brain doesn't get too tired. When you **save your energy for the big decisions,** you'll make **better choices all day long!**

Chapter 35: Stress-Reduction Techniques – How to Stay Calm Under Pressure

Have you ever felt **so stressed** about making a decision that you just **froze** and couldn't decide at all? Maybe you had to pick a topic for a school project, but you felt overwhelmed by all the options. Or maybe you had to decide which team to join, and the pressure made you nervous.

When you're **stressed out**, it's **harder to think clearly**—and that can lead to bad decisions. That's why learning **how to stay calm** can help you make **better choices, even in tough situations.**

Why Stress Makes Decision-Making Harder

When you feel stressed, your brain **goes into panic mode.** Instead of thinking things through, you might:

- **Rush into a decision** just to get it over with. (*Example: Picking a random science project instead of one you actually like.*)

- **Avoid deciding at all** because it feels too overwhelming. (*Example: Not choosing a summer activity and missing the deadline to sign up!*)
- **Make choices based on fear** instead of logic. (*Example: Skipping a big opportunity because you're afraid of failing.*)

How to Stay Calm and Make Better Choices

Instead of letting stress take over, try these simple tricks to **calm your brain before making a decision:**

1. **Take a deep breath.** When you're stressed, your brain speeds up. Taking a deep breath helps you **slow down and think clearly.**

2. **Break big decisions into small steps.** Instead of thinking *"I have to decide everything right now,"* start with the **first step** and go from there.

3. **Ask for help.** Sometimes talking to a friend, parent, or teacher can **help you see your choices more clearly.**

4. **Take a short break.** If a decision is making you **too stressed**, step away for a few minutes. A quick walk or listening to music can help clear your mind.

5. **Remind yourself that no decision is perfect.** You don't have to make the *perfect* choice—just the best one for you at the moment.

Try It Yourself!

Imagine you're feeling **stressed about picking a club to join at school.**

- **Without stress control:** You panic, pick the first club you see, and later realize it's not what you wanted.
- **With stress control:** You take a deep breath, look at your options, and **choose the club that fits your interests best.**

How to Make Choices Without Feeling Stuck

Stress can make decision-making feel **overwhelming,** but the trick is to **slow down, breathe, and take small steps.** When you **stay calm, you think more clearly**—and that helps you make **better choices, no matter the situation!**

Chapter 36: The Pause Principle – Stop, Breathe, and Think Before You Act

Have you ever **answered too quickly** and then realized you said the wrong thing? Or agreed to something **before thinking it through** and later wished you had chosen differently?

That's why the **Pause Principle** is so important! It's a simple trick that helps you **stop, think, and make a better choice—** instead of rushing into a decision you might regret.

Why Rushing Leads to Bad Decisions

Your brain **wants to decide fast**, but quick choices aren't always smart ones.

- **You say "yes" to something you don't want to do** just because you feel pressured.
- **You send a text when you're mad** and regret it later.
- **You pick the first answer on a test** without reading the question carefully.

How the Pause Principle Works

Before making a decision, **pause for a moment** and ask yourself:

1. **Do I really want to do this?** (*Or am I just saying yes because I feel pressured?*)
2. **Will I regret this choice later?** (*If I take a second to think, will I pick something better?*)
3. **What happens next?** (*If I say this, do this, or choose this, how will it affect me?*)

Try It Yourself!

Imagine your friend **dares you to do something silly in front of a big crowd.**

- **Without pausing:** You say yes immediately, but later feel embarrassed.
- **With the Pause Principle:** You stop and think, *Do I actually want to do this?* You decide to say no and feel much better about your choice.

Why This Works

The Pause Principle helps you:

- Avoid bad decisions that come from pressure or emotions.
- Think before you act, so you don't regret your choice later.
- Feel more confident about the decisions you make.

A Simple Trick to Make Smarter Choices

Next time you're about to **make a quick decision**, stop for a second. **That tiny pause can help you avoid mistakes, stay in control, and make choices you'll feel good about later!**

Chapter 37: Handling Regret – Learning from Mistakes Without Feeling Bad Forever

Have you ever made a decision and later thought, **"I wish I had chosen differently"**? Maybe you spent all your money on a toy and then saw something even cooler the next day. Or maybe you said something unkind in an argument and felt bad afterward.

That feeling is called **regret**—and everyone experiences it sometimes. The good news? **Regret can actually help you make better choices in the future—if you handle it the right way!**

Why Do People Feel Regret?

Regret happens when you realize:

- **You made a choice too quickly.** (*Example: You rushed to pick a snack and later wished you had chosen something better.*)

- **You ignored your gut feeling.** (*Example: You felt unsure about skipping practice but did it anyway—and later regretted it.*)
- **You acted on emotions instead of thinking it through.** (*Example: You yelled at a friend and later wished you had stayed calm.*)

What to Do When You Feel Regret

Instead of feeling **stuck** in regret, use it as a chance to **learn and grow.**

1. **Accept that everyone makes mistakes.** Even the smartest people in the world make choices they later regret.
2. **Ask yourself, "What can I learn from this?"** If you regret something, think about how you can make a better choice next time.
3. **Apologize if you need to.** If your decision hurt someone else, saying sorry can **help fix the situation** and make you both feel better.
4. **Move forward.** Regret is only helpful if you use it to make better choices. Once you've learned your lesson, let it go and focus on what's next!

Try It Yourself!

Imagine you **forgot to study for a test and got a bad grade.**

- **Feeling stuck in regret:** You keep thinking, *I'm terrible at this. I should have studied!* but don't do anything to change it.
- **Using regret to grow:** You say, *Next time, I'll plan ahead and study a little each day!*

How to Turn Regret into a Lesson

Regret **doesn't have to be a bad thing**—it can actually **make you a smarter decision-maker!** The next time you make a mistake, don't just feel bad about it. **Ask yourself what you can learn, make a plan to do better, and move forward with confidence!**

Chapter 38: Making Peace with Uncertainty – Accepting That You Can't Know Everything

Have you ever had to make a decision but **felt unsure** because you didn't have all the answers? Maybe you were picking a new activity to try but weren't sure if you'd like it. Or maybe you were deciding whether to introduce yourself to someone new but didn't know how they would react.

That feeling of **not knowing everything** is called **uncertainty**—and it's completely normal! No one can predict the future, but that doesn't mean you should avoid making decisions. Learning to **make peace with uncertainty** helps you **move forward with confidence, even when you don't have all the answers.**

Why Uncertainty Feels Uncomfortable

Your brain **likes knowing things for sure**, so when there are unknowns, you might feel:

- **Worried about making the wrong choice.** (*What if I pick the wrong activity and don't like it?*)

- **Afraid of failure.** (*What if I try and don't do well?*)
- **Stuck and unable to decide.** (*Maybe I just won't choose at all!*)

But here's the truth: **Most great decisions happen even when you don't know everything!**

How to Make Good Decisions Even When You're Unsure

Instead of waiting until you have **every single answer**, try these strategies:

1. **Gather what information you can.** (*Example: If you're picking a club to join, ask someone who's already in it what it's like!*)

2. **Accept that some things are unknown.** (*Example: You won't know if you love a new activity until you try it—and that's okay!*)

3. **Take a small step instead of a big leap.** (*Example: If you're unsure about a new hobby, try it once before fully committing!*)

Try It Yourself!

Imagine you're deciding **whether to enter a competition.**

- **Getting stuck in uncertainty:** You think, *What if I'm not good enough? What if I don't win?* So, you decide not to try at all.

- **Making peace with uncertainty:** You think, *I don't know what will happen, but I can try my best and learn from the experience.*

Why It's Okay Not to Know Everything

No one can predict the future, but that shouldn't stop you from making decisions. Instead of feeling stuck, **accept that some things are unknown**—and make the best choice you can with what you do know! The more you practice, the easier it gets to **trust yourself, even when things feel uncertain.**

SECTION VI
Making Decisions with Others

Not every decision is just about **you** — sometimes, you have to make choices **with other people.** Whether it's deciding what game to play with friends, working on a school project, or solving a disagreement, learning how to **listen, share ideas, and work as a team** is super important. In this section, you'll learn how to **make group decisions that are fair, smart, and keep everyone happy!**

Chapter 39: Consensus-Building – Getting a Group to Agree

Have you ever been in a group where **no one could agree on what to do?** Maybe one friend wanted to play soccer, another wanted to play tag, and someone else wanted to just sit and talk. How do you make a decision that **everyone** feels good about?

That's where **consensus-building** comes in! It's a way of making decisions where **everyone shares their ideas, listens to each other, and works together to find the best choice.** Instead of one person deciding for the whole group, **everyone gets a say.**

How Consensus-Building Works

Instead of arguing or just doing what the loudest person wants, you follow these simple steps:

1. **Listen to everyone's ideas.** Each person shares what they think, and everyone listens without interrupting.
2. **Find common ground.** Look for something **most people agree on.**

3. **Talk through the options.** If people disagree, see if there's a way to **combine ideas** or find a middle ground.

4. **Make a final decision that feels fair.** Everyone might not get exactly what they want, but **no one should feel ignored or left out.**

Let's Try It!

Imagine your group is trying to **pick a movie for a sleepover.**

- **One person wants a funny movie.**
- **Another wants an action movie.**
- **Someone else wants a cartoon.**

Instead of arguing, you could:

- Find a movie that has both action and comedy.
- Take a vote and let the group decide.
- Plan to watch one type of movie this time and a different one next time.

Now, instead of **one person being unhappy,** everyone feels included!

Why This Works

Consensus-building helps you:

- **Make group decisions without arguing.**
- **Make sure everyone's voice is heard.**
- **Find solutions that work for everyone, not just one person.**

How to Make Group Decisions Without Fighting

The next time you and your friends or family **can't agree on something**, try using consensus-building. **When everyone feels included in the decision, people are happier, and things go much more smoothly!**

Chapter 40: Avoiding Power Dynamics – When Someone Bossy Takes Over

Have you ever been in a group where **one person made all the decisions** without listening to anyone else? Maybe a bossy friend chose the game without asking what others wanted. Or maybe a loud classmate took over a group project while everyone else just followed along.

This is called a **power dynamic** — when one person has **more control over a decision than everyone else.** It can make choices feel **unfair** and leave others feeling ignored. But good decision-making means **everyone's voice should count!**

Why Power Dynamics Can Be a Problem

When one person takes over, group decisions can go wrong:

- **Some people feel left out.** (*Example: A leader picks the game, but half the group doesn't want to play.*)

- **Others just go along with it, even if they don't agree.** (*Example: A classmate makes all the decisions for a project, but no one else speaks up.*)

- **It's not really a fair choice.** (*Example: A coach always picks the same players first, even if others deserve a turn.*)

How to Make Sure Everyone's Voice Counts

Instead of letting **one person** control the decision, try these fair ways to decide:

1. **Take turns leading.** If your group makes decisions often, let a different person lead each time.

2. **Use voting.** If there are two or three choices, let everyone vote so the majority decides.

3. **Ask for opinions.** Before deciding, go around the group and let everyone share their thoughts.

4. **Make sure quiet people get a chance to speak.** Some people don't like to talk over others, so check in with them.

Try It Yourself!

Imagine your friend group is picking a game, but one person **always chooses what they want** without asking anyone else.

- **With power dynamics:** That person picks, and others don't get a say.

- **Without power dynamics:** Everyone suggests a game, and the group votes or takes turns choosing.

How to Make Group Decisions Fair for Everyone

A good group decision **doesn't let one person take over**—it makes sure **everyone gets a voice.** The next time you're making a choice with others, **be fair, listen to everyone, and make sure no one feels ignored!**

Chapter 41: The Wisdom of Crowds – When More People Make a Smarter Choice

Have you ever noticed that **big decisions** are often made by groups instead of just one person? Schools have student councils, governments have teams of leaders, and game shows let the audience help answer tough questions.

That's because of something called **the wisdom of crowds** — the idea that **a group of people, thinking together, often makes a better decision than one person alone.** When different people **share their ideas and knowledge**, the group can **see the full picture and make a smarter choice.**

Why Groups Make Smarter Decisions

No one person **knows everything**, but when people **combine their knowledge**, they can:

- **Catch mistakes that one person might miss.** (*Example: One student might forget part of a project, but another remembers it!*)

- **Come up with more creative ideas.** (*Example: A team brainstorming together can think of better solutions than just one person alone.*)
  - **Balance different opinions.** (*Example: If one person wants a risky choice, others might suggest a safer option.*)

When Groups Make Bad Decisions

Groups don't always get it right. Sometimes, they can be **wrong together** if:

- **Everyone copies what others say without thinking for themselves.** (*Example: If one person shouts an answer, others might agree just to fit in—even if it's wrong!*)
- **People don't share their true opinions.** (*Example: Someone might have a great idea but stay quiet because they're nervous.*)
- **The group follows the loudest person instead of listening to all voices.**

How to Use the Wisdom of Crowds the Right Way

To make good group decisions, follow these steps:

1. **Get different opinions.** Ask people with different experiences and ideas to share their thoughts.
2. **Think for yourself, too.** Just because the group is choosing something doesn't mean it's automatically right—double-check the facts.
3. **Make sure everyone speaks up.** Sometimes, the best ideas come from the quietest voices.

Try It Yourself!

Imagine your class is guessing **how many jellybeans are in a jar.**

- **One person guesses alone:** They might be way off.
- **A whole class guesses together:** By averaging everyone's guesses, the group gets much closer to the right answer!

The **wisdom of crowds** works best when **everyone shares their ideas and listens to each other.** The next time you have a big decision, try **asking a group of people for their opinions—you might end up with a much better choice than you could have made alone!**

Chapter 42: The Delphi Technique – Getting Advice the Right Way

Have you ever been in a group where people **argued so much that no decision was made at all**? Maybe your class tried to pick a field trip location, but everyone shouted their opinions, and nothing got decided. Or maybe your team was choosing a name, but no one could agree because everyone wanted their own idea to win.

That's where **the Delphi Technique** comes in! It's a smart way to **help groups make better decisions** without arguing. Instead of letting the loudest person take over, this method lets **everyone share their ideas in a fair and organized way.**

How the Delphi Technique Works

Instead of **arguing in a big discussion**, the group follows these steps:

1. **Everyone writes down their ideas separately.** This way, no one is influenced by others.

2. **A leader collects the answers and shares them anonymously.** That means no one knows whose idea is whose.

3. **Everyone looks at all the ideas and gives feedback.** The group discusses which ideas are the best and why.

4. **The group votes or revises ideas until they reach the best decision.**

By doing it this way, people **think carefully instead of just going along with the crowd**, and quieter voices get heard too!

Why This Works

The Delphi Technique helps groups:

- **Avoid arguments** by letting people share their ideas in a calmer way.

- **Think deeply** instead of just choosing the first idea that pops up.

- **Make fairer decisions** because no one's opinion is ignored.

Try It Yourself!

Imagine your class is trying to decide **what to do for a school fundraiser.**

- **Without the Delphi Technique:** The loudest students argue, and some kids don't even get a chance to share their ideas.

- **With the Delphi Technique:** Everyone writes their ideas down, all ideas are shared fairly, and the best one is chosen based on what works best for the whole group.

A Better Way to Make Group Decisions

The Delphi Technique **helps groups make decisions without pressure, arguing, or unfairness.** Next time you're in a group that can't agree, suggest **writing down ideas first—you** might be surprised at how much smoother things go!

Chapter 43: Role Assignment – Giving Everyone a Job in Group Decisions

Have you ever been in a group project where **one person did all the work** while others just sat around? Or maybe **everyone tried to lead at the same time**, and it turned into a big mess?

That's why **Role Assignment** is important! It means **giving each person in the group a specific job** so that everything gets done **fairly and efficiently.** When everyone knows their role, the group works together smoothly—and decisions are made without chaos.

Why Role Assignment Helps

When a group doesn't assign roles:

- **Some people do everything, while others do nothing.** (*Example: One student writes the whole project while the rest just watch.*)

- **Everyone tries to be in charge, leading to arguments.** (*Example: Two people try to be the leader, and they keep disagreeing on what to do next.*)

- **Important details get forgotten.** (*Example: The group picks a great idea but forgets to check if it's even possible.*)

When **everyone has a role**, work gets done faster, **everyone feels included**, and decisions are made more easily.

Common Roles in Group Decisions

Depending on the situation, different roles might be needed. Here are a few examples:

1. **The Leader** – Helps keep the group focused and makes sure everyone is included.

2. **The Researcher** – Looks up important facts or information to help make a smart choice.

3. **The Organizer** – Makes a plan for how to get things done step by step.

4. **The Question-Asker** – Challenges ideas by asking, *"Did we think of everything?"*

5. **The Speaker** – Shares the group's decision with others once it's made.

By **dividing responsibilities**, everyone has a part to play, and no one feels left out.

Try It Yourself!

Imagine your class is **planning a talent show.**

- **Without Role Assignment:** Everyone argues about what to do, and no one is sure who is in charge.

- **With Role Assignment:** One person leads, another organizes sign-ups, another handles decorations, and another makes sure all acts are scheduled. Everything runs smoothly!

A Simple Way to Make Group Decisions Work Better

Next time you're in a group, try **assigning roles.** When everyone has a job, **decisions happen faster, work gets done fairly, and the group succeeds as a team!**

Chapter 44: Encouraging Constructive Dissent – Speaking Up When You Disagree

Have you ever been in a group where everyone agreed on something, but you **weren't so sure** it was the best idea? Maybe your friends wanted to take a shortcut on a hike, but you thought it looked unsafe. Or maybe your class picked a project idea that didn't make sense, but no one wanted to say anything.

It can feel uncomfortable to **disagree with a group**, but sometimes **speaking up is the right thing to do.** That's called **constructive dissent**—when you share a different opinion in a way that helps the group **think more carefully and make a better decision.**

When people **never question an idea**, mistakes can happen.

- **A team picks the first idea without thinking it through** – Later, they realize it wasn't the best option.

- **A group follows a risky plan** – No one speaks up, even though someone had doubts.

- **People agree just to fit in** – This is when people go along with something just because they don't want to be different.

How to Disagree the Right Way

Sharing a different opinion **doesn't mean arguing or being rude**—it means **helping the group see other possibilities.** Here's how to do it the right way:

1. **Stay respectful.** Instead of saying, *"That's a bad idea,"* try, *"I see it differently—can I share my thoughts?"*

2. **Explain your reason.** Say why you disagree and give a clear example.

3. **Suggest an alternative.** Instead of just saying no, offer a new idea that might work better.

Try It Yourself!

Imagine your group is **choosing a fundraiser idea**, and they all want to sell something expensive.

- **Staying silent:** You know some people can't afford it, but you don't say anything. The fundraiser doesn't go well.

- **Using constructive dissent:** You say, *"That's a cool idea, but what if we also sell something more affordable so everyone can participate?"* Now, the group has a better plan!

Why Disagreeing Can Lead to Smarter Choices

Speaking up when something **doesn't seem right** can help **prevent mistakes, improve ideas, and make sure everyone is included.** The next time you're in a group, **don't be afraid to share a different perspective—it might just lead to the best decision!**

Chapter 45: Accountability in Groups – Taking Responsibility for Decisions

Have you ever been in a group where **someone didn't do their part**? Maybe your class was working on a poster, but one person forgot their job, and everyone else had to fix it. Or maybe your team was supposed to clean up after an event, but some people left early, and others had to do extra work.

When people don't **take responsibility**, it can lead to frustration, unfinished work, and bad decisions. But when everyone **does their part and owns up to their actions**, the group works better — and things turn out great!

Why Taking Responsibility Matters

When no one takes responsibility, problems happen:

- **Things don't get done.** (*Example: The group plans a bake sale, but no one brings the supplies!*)
- **People get blamed.** (*Example: A mistake happens, but instead of fixing it, everyone just argues about whose fault it was.*)

- **Some people do all the work.** (*Example: A few kids finish a project while others just sit back and watch.*)

But when everyone **does their part**, groups can **make better decisions and work as a real team!**

How to Be Responsible in a Group

1. **Keep your promises.** If you say you'll do something, make sure you actually do it.
2. **Speak up if you make a mistake.** If you forgot something or need help, tell the group so you can fix it together.
3. **Check in with each other.** Ask, *"Does everyone have what they need?"* before it's too late.
4. **Give credit to everyone.** If the group does well, celebrate together instead of letting one person take all the credit.

Try It Yourself!

Imagine your class is working on **a play for school.**

- **Without accountability:** One person forgets their lines but doesn't practice, so the whole scene gets messed up.
- **With accountability:** They admit they need help, and the group helps them rehearse. The play turns out great!

Why Responsibility Makes Teams Stronger

When everyone in a group **takes responsibility**, things get done faster, decisions are fairer, and the whole team **feels proud of their work.** The next time you're in a group, **do your part, be honest, and help each other out—that's how great teams make great choices!**

SECTION VII
Thinking Ahead for the Future

Making decisions isn't just about **what's happening right now** — some choices affect your future, too! The decisions you make today can shape **what happens tomorrow, next week, or even years from now.** That's why learning to **think ahead** is so important. In this section, you'll discover smart ways to **plan for the future, avoid big mistakes, and make choices that help you succeed in the long run!**

Chapter 46: Game Theory Basics – Making the Best Move in Every Situation

Have you ever played a game where you had to **think ahead to win**? Maybe in chess, you planned your next few moves before making them. Or in tag, you predicted where your friend would run so you could tag them faster.

That's exactly how **Game Theory** works! It's all about **thinking ahead, predicting what others will do, and making the smartest move based on that.**

How Game Theory Works

Game Theory helps you **make better choices** by asking:

1. **What do I want to happen?** (*Example: I want to win this board game.*)

2. **What might the other person do?** (*Example: My opponent will probably block my next move.*)

3. **What's the smartest move based on that?** (*Example: I'll plan two steps ahead so they can't stop me!*)

It's like playing a **strategy game in real life!**

Game Theory in Everyday Life

Game Theory doesn't just work in games—it helps with real-life decisions too!

- **Taking turns:** If you always grab the best seat, your friends might stop letting you pick first. But if you take turns, everyone stays happy.
- **Negotiating:** If you and your sibling both want the last cookie, you can **offer to split it** instead of arguing and both getting in trouble.
- **Teamwork:** If you're playing soccer, **passing the ball at the right time** makes your team stronger instead of just trying to score alone.

Try It Yourself!

Imagine you and a friend are picking a movie to watch.

- **Without Game Theory:** You demand to watch what you want, but your friend refuses, and no one gets to watch anything.
- **With Game Theory:** You think ahead and say, *"Let's watch my choice today and your choice next time."* Now, both of you are happy!

Why Thinking Ahead Helps You Win

Game Theory **teaches you to predict what will happen next** so you can make the smartest choice. Whether you're playing a game, solving a problem, or working with others, **thinking ahead helps you succeed!**

Chapter 47: The Long View – Thinking About How Your Choices Affect the Future

Have you ever rushed through something just to get it over with, only to **wish you had taken more time**? Maybe you **scribbled down answers on a worksheet** just to finish quickly, but later you got them wrong. Or maybe you **picked the first idea for a project** instead of thinking it through, and later realized a different idea would have been much better.

That's why it's important to take **the long view**—which means **thinking beyond right now** and asking, *"How will this decision affect me later?"*

Why Quick and Easy Choices Aren't Always the Best

Some choices **feel like a good idea at the moment**, but later you might wish you had thought ahead.

- **Rushing through a test just to finish early** – You might make silly mistakes that you wouldn't have made if you had checked your work.

- **Picking the easiest book for a reading assignment** – You finish fast, but later you realize you didn't enjoy it or learn anything new.
- **Choosing not to practice for a big game** – You save time in the moment, but later you feel unprepared when it's time to play.

How to Think About the Future Before Deciding

Next time you have a choice to make, ask yourself:

1. **Will I still be happy with this decision tomorrow?** (*Example: If I rush through my project, will I be proud of my work later?*)
2. **Will this choice help me later on?** (*Example: If I practice a little each day, will I feel more confident when it really matters?*)
3. **If I take a little more time now, will it make things easier later?** (*Example: If I organize my backpack today, will I save time searching for things tomorrow?*)

Try It Yourself!

Imagine you're **building a puzzle.**

- **Short-term thinking:** You force the pieces together quickly, but they don't fit right, and you have to start over.
- **Long-term thinking:** You take your time and find the right pieces, so the puzzle comes together perfectly.

Why Thinking Ahead Helps You Succeed

When you take **the long view**, you make choices that **don't just feel good right now but also help you later.** Next time you're making a decision, **think beyond today—your future self will thank you!**

Chapter 48: Scenario Thinking – Imagining Different Futures Before You Decide

Have you ever watched someone **make a bad decision that could have been avoided** if they had just thought ahead? Maybe a friend signed up for too many activities and later felt overwhelmed, or someone started a big project without planning and ran out of time.

That's where **Scenario Thinking** helps! It's a way to **imagine different possibilities before making a choice** so you can avoid problems and prepare for success.

How Scenario Thinking Works

Before making a decision, ask yourself:

1. **What's the best thing that could happen?** (*Example: If I prepare for my speech, I'll feel confident and do well.*)

2. **What's the worst thing that could happen?** (*Example: If I don't practice, I might forget what to say and feel embarrassed.*)

3. **What's the most likely thing to happen?** (*Example: If I spend time practicing, I'll do fine, even if I feel a little nervous.*)

Why Scenario Thinking Helps You Make Smarter Choices

By imagining different possibilities, you can:

- **Avoid last-minute stress** by planning ahead.
- **Be better prepared** for challenges that might come up.
- **Make a choice that works for both now and later.**

Try It Yourself!

Imagine you're deciding **whether to join a new club at school.**

- **Best-case scenario:** You enjoy it, make new friends, and learn something cool.
- **Worst-case scenario:** It takes up too much time, and you struggle to keep up with your other work.
- **Most likely scenario:** If you manage your time wisely, you can participate and still balance your responsibilities.

A Smart Way to Plan for the Future

Scenario Thinking **helps you think ahead so you're ready for whatever happens.** The next time you're making a choice, **take a moment to picture different outcomes — so you can make the best decision possible!**

Chapter 49: Strategic Patience – Why Waiting Can Lead to Better Decisions

Have you ever been in a hurry to decide something, only to **wish you had waited a little longer**? Maybe you picked a book from the library quickly, but later found one you liked even more. Or maybe you answered a question in class too fast and realized **you knew a better answer** after thinking about it for a few more seconds.

That's where **Strategic Patience** helps! It means **waiting when it's the smart thing to do** — not because you're avoiding a decision, but because **a better choice might come if you give yourself time to think.**

Why Rushing Can Lead to Mistakes

Sometimes, making a quick decision **feels good in the moment** but doesn't work out in the long run.

- **Choosing the first idea that pops into your head** – You might come up with a better one if you take a little more time.

- **Answering a question too fast** – If you wait and think, you might remember something more accurate.
- **Saying "yes" to something without thinking** – You might realize later that you **don't actually have the time** or **don't really want to do it.**

How to Use Strategic Patience the Right Way

Strategic Patience **doesn't mean waiting forever** — it means knowing when to **pause and think before making a choice.**

1. **If a decision isn't urgent, give yourself time.** (*Example: If you're picking a book, take a few minutes to check different options before choosing.*)

2. **Ask yourself, "Do I really need to decide right now?"** (*Example: If someone asks for a favor, think about your schedule before saying yes immediately.*)

3. **Use waiting time wisely.** (*Example: If you're waiting to make a big decision, use the time to gather more information instead of just hoping for the best.*)

Try It Yourself!

Imagine you're deciding **which topic to choose for a school project.**

- **Without Strategic Patience:** You pick the first idea that comes to mind, but later realize it's not that interesting.

- **With Strategic Patience:** You take time to explore different topics and find one that's **really exciting and fun to work on.**

Why Waiting Can Lead to Smarter Choices

Strategic Patience **helps you avoid rushing into decisions you might regret.** The next time you have a choice to make, **pause and give yourself time to think—you might come up with a much better idea!**

Chapter 50: The Power of Experimentation – Testing Your Choices Before Committing

Have you ever wished you could **try something out before making a big decision**? What if you could test a sport before joining the team, or try out an instrument before committing to lessons? That's exactly what **experimentation** is all about!

Instead of guessing or making a choice you're unsure about, **experimentation lets you test things first** so you can make a smarter decision.

Why Experimenting Helps You Make Better Choices

Sometimes, it's hard to know if a choice is right until you've **actually tried it.**

- **Trying out a new hobby** – Instead of signing up for a whole season, you attend a trial class first.

- **Testing a new study method** – Before changing how you study, you try it for one test to see if it helps.

- **Exploring different interests** – Instead of assuming you won't like something, you give it a short try before deciding.

How to Use Experimentation in Decision-Making

Before making a big decision, ask yourself:

1. **Can I test this first before committing?** (*Example: If I'm unsure about joining a club, can I go to one meeting first?*)

2. **What small step can I take to see if this works?** (*Example: If I want to start running, can I try short runs before training for a race?*)

3. **How do I feel after trying it?** (*Example: Do I actually enjoy this, or do I want to try something else?*)

Try It Yourself!

Imagine you're deciding **whether to volunteer for a big event.**

- **Without Experimentation:** You sign up for a big role right away and later realize it's too much work.

- **With Experimentation:** You help out for a short time first, then decide whether you want to take on a bigger role.

Trust experience

Experimentation **helps you make decisions based on more than just guesses.** The next time you're unsure about something, **test it out first — then decide if it's right for you!**

Conclusion: What Makes a Great Decision-Maker? How to Keep Practicing Every Day!

By now, you've learned **so many ways** to make smart choices! You know how to **think ahead, stay calm, listen to others, and take responsibility** for your decisions. But the most important thing to remember is this: **Good decision-making is a skill—you get better at it the more you practice!**

What Great Decision-Makers Do

1. **They don't rush.** They **pause and think** before making a choice.
2. **They look at different options.** Instead of just picking the first idea, they **consider all the possibilities.**
3. **They ask for advice when needed.** They're not afraid to **listen and learn from others.**
4. **They aren't afraid of mistakes.** They know that **every choice is a chance to learn and improve.**

The more you **practice these skills in everyday life,** the easier it will be to make smart choices — big and small!

How to Keep Practicing

- **Play the "what if" game.** Ask yourself, *"What might happen if I make this choice?"*
- **Pause before deciding.** Give yourself a moment to think before jumping to a decision.
- **Learn from past choices.** If something didn't go well, think about what you could do differently next time.

Remember, **no one makes perfect choices all the time.** What matters most is that you keep **learning, thinking, and making the best choices you can!**

Appendices

1. Quick Reference Guide – A Cheat Sheet for Smart Decision-Making

Here's a **quick reminder** of the best tricks for making great choices!

Before You Decide, Ask Yourself:

What are my options? (*Is there more than one choice?*)

What could happen next? (*What are the good and bad results of each choice?*)

How will this choice affect me later? (*Will I still be happy with this decision tomorrow?*)

Am I feeling too emotional to decide? (*Should I take a break and think it over?*)

Do I need more information? (*Should I ask someone for advice?*)

If You're in a Group Decision:

Is everyone getting a chance to speak?

Are we thinking about all the options?

Are we choosing fairly, not just going with the loudest person's idea?

If You Make a Mistake:

What can I learn from this?

How can I make a better choice next time?

2. Practice Scenarios for Kids – Spot the Decision-Making Mistake Game!

Test your decision-making skills! Read each situation, find the mistake, and see how it can be fixed.

Scenario 1: The Rushed Choice

Liam is in a hurry to finish his homework, so he writes random answers without checking them. The next day, he realizes he made a lot of mistakes.

What went wrong?

Liam rushed through his work without taking time to check his answers, leading to mistakes.

Better choice:

Liam should slow down and take a few extra minutes to review his work. Even a quick check at the end can help catch mistakes and improve his answers.

Scenario 2: Ignoring Other Ideas

Samantha and her friends are picking a movie. Samantha insists on her choice and doesn't listen to anyone else. Some friends aren't happy.

What went wrong?

Samantha didn't consider what her friends wanted, which made the decision unfair.

Better choice:

Samantha should ask everyone for their opinions and look for a fair way to decide, like voting or taking turns choosing the movie.

Scenario 3: Not Thinking Ahead

Jordan spends all his free time playing outside and forgets to study for his test. When the test comes, he doesn't know the answers.

What went wrong?

Jordan didn't plan his time well and left his studying until it was too late.

Better choice:

Jordan should set aside a little time each day to review his notes. That way, he can still have fun outside while also being ready for the test.

Scenario 4: Letting Emotions Take Over

Mia is upset because her brother borrowed her markers without asking. She yells at him and takes one of his toys in return. Later, she feels bad.

What went wrong?

Mia reacted out of anger instead of solving the problem calmly.

Better choice:

Mia should take a deep breath and talk to her brother about how she feels. She can tell him why it upset her and ask him to ask permission next time.

Scenario 5: Making a Decision Without Enough Information

Ethan sees a cool-looking book at the library and checks it out without reading the summary or looking inside. When he gets home, he realizes he doesn't like it.

What went wrong?

Ethan picked a book without checking if it was something he would enjoy.

Better choice:

Ethan should take a moment to read the back cover or a few pages before choosing. This helps make sure the book is interesting to him.

Scenario 6: Avoiding Responsibility

Sophia is in a group project, but she forgets to do her part and doesn't tell her teammates. On the day of the presentation, the group is unprepared.

What went wrong?

Sophia didn't take responsibility for her task, which hurt the whole group.

Better choice:

Sophia should have let her team know she needed help or set a reminder to complete her part on time. When everyone in a group does their share, the project turns out better.

Scenario 7: Ignoring a Possible Problem

David and his friends are planning a picnic. The forecast says it might rain, but they don't make a backup plan. When it starts raining, they don't know what to do.

What went wrong?

David and his friends didn't prepare for the possibility of rain, which left them stuck.

Better choice:

They should have thought ahead and picked an indoor backup plan, like eating lunch in a covered area or at someone's house. Thinking about different outcomes helps avoid surprises.

3. Tips for Decision-Making – The Top 10 Tricks for Choosing Wisely

1. **Take a deep breath before deciding.** (*A quick pause helps you think clearly!*)
2. **List your choices.** (*There's always more than one option!*)
3. **Think about what could happen next.** (*Good and bad results matter!*)
4. **Ask yourself: Will I still be happy with this choice later?**
5. **If it's a big decision, get advice from someone you trust.**
6. **If you're in a group, make sure everyone's voice is heard.**
7. **Use the "what if" test.** (*What if I wait? What if I choose differently?*)
8. **Don't let emotions take over.** (*If you're too angry, excited, or upset, wait before deciding!*)
9. **If you make a mistake, learn from it.** (*Mistakes are just lessons for next time!*)
10. **Practice, practice, practice!** (*The more you use these skills, the better you'll get!*)

Final Thought

Every day, you make **hundreds of decisions.** Some are small, like what to eat or wear. Others are big, like how to handle a challenge or solve a problem. No matter what the decision is, using these **smart decision-making skills** will help you **think clearly, make better choices, and feel more confident about the future!**

Here's another book by Quinn Voss that you might like